Jewish Cooking Secrets
From Here & Far

Traditions & Memories from Our Mothers' Kitchens

Edited & Compiled by Lorraine Gerstl

SAMUEL
WACHTMAN'S
SONS

An Imprint of the Millennium Publishing Group

Distributed to the book trade by Summit Publishing Group

©1996 by The Millennium Publishing Group

No portion of this book may be reproduced in any form without written permission from the publisher, The Millennium Publishing Group, 1271 Tenth Street, Monterey, California 93940. If unavailable in local bookstores, additional copies of this and other publications of the Millennium Publishing Group may be purchased by writing the Publisher at the above address.

Library of Congress Cataloging-in-Publication Data
    Gerstl, Lorraine
    Jewish Cooking Secrets—From Here and Far
    Lorraine Gerstl
    Batik Cover Art by Amos Amit
    192 p. cm.
    CIP No.
    ISBN 1-88882-001-2
    1. Cooking
    2. Jewish Cooking
    3. Jewish Customs
    II. Title

Cover by Morris Design, Monterey, California
Interior by Electra Typography, San Francisco, California
Map of Jewish Eastern Europe adapted from The Shtetl Book by David J. Roskies and Diane K. Roskies. ©1975 by Ktav Publishing House, Inc. Used by permission of David Roskies

Printed in the United States of America

2 4 6 8 9 7 5 3 1

With special thanks to my co-editors
Zelma Weinfield, Ettie Buch, Shelli Klein
and, of course, to my beloved Hugo

JEWISH EASTERN EUROPE
1830-1914

⊛ Provincial Capital   ★ Major City   • Settlement

—··—··— Border   ·············· Provincial Border

▨▨ Congress Poland   ▨▨ Pale of Settlement

Contents

Introduction

Once upon a time, a young man named Moishele left his home and family in the old country and started a search for his fortune in the form of diamonds. His journey was unsuccessful, and decades later he returned home. His parents had passed away; his fiancée had married another and was now a grandmother. He was grievously saddened by the failure of his life's mission.

His abandoned home was still standing, and so, sadly, he lay down to sleep the sleep of the weary and the disillusioned. When he awoke, he went outside, as was his habit, to dig for diamonds, just as he had done each morning of his sad and lonely life in all the countries of the world that he had searched. And lo and behold—there they were, in his own backyard!

This home is the mythic home of the Jew. Some do not appreciate it while still in it and adventure far and wide to find diamonds of many sorts; on returning, they discover all the nourishment and riches necessary for life. Jews have lived the world over, in varied circumstances—often in extreme adversity and poverty—but the home was always a place of sustenance and enrichment and the sharing of love and family.

The latter has been the means through which traditional Jewish celebrations have survived and flourished—and most of these festivities and rituals that enhance and unify the family are centered around the kitchen. In this spirit, and aware of the treasures that our traditional foods offer, we proudly present this cookbook—a "first" in the already popular Secrets series.

The original concept of this book came from Congregation Beth Israel, a diverse congregation whose members hailed from as far away as Russia, Lithuania, South Africa, Australia, and virtually every state in the United States. It was edited by Joyce Kurtz, Heather Mendel and Karen Wiskoff, to whom I am greatly indebted. From there, we expanded to obtain recipes from many sources, including delicatessens and Kosher restaurants throughout North America and distinguished Jewish "home chefs" in places as geographically distant as Cape Town, Vienna and London.

The recipes in this book may not have been laboratory tested, but their merit has been established by the most critical groups of all—our families. They reflect not only our past, but an awareness today of health issues that were not considered in times past, when people were only concerned about having enough food for survival and being able to stretch their meager portions to feed large families. In compiling a cookbook such as this, we could start by asking the question, "What is Jewish cooking?" Trying to answer this question is nearly as daunting a task as trying to answer the question, "What is a Jew?" A trite answer is that Jewish food is whatever Jews eat, and Jewish cooking is however they prepare it.

Just as Judaism has always been influenced by the places and times in which Jews find themselves, so, too, the food we eat, the way we prepare it carries remembrances of the places our ancestors have been. These places are far and varied. We are aware of the presence of our ancestors in Europe, both north and south, the Middle East, Australia and South Africa over the last centuries, but we now know of Jews in India dating back before the Common Era, and have records of a distinguished Jewish community, Kai Feng, China from the time of the Sung Dynasty in 979. For Jews, in all times and places, the preparation and sharing of food has been and continues to be a very important part of our family life. This is reflected in our teachings: *"You should eat and be full and you shall bless...."*

As we wish to teach our children of the privilege of having food and making mealtimes sacred, traditionally we sing or recite the blessing, HaMotsi, over bread before each meal and over the specially braided challah for the Shabbat. An important part of the Shabbat and festival meals too, is wine over which we chant our thanks for the fruit of the vine. Each meal is concluded with the Birkat HaMazon—a prayer of thanksgiving for the meal just ended.

In this country, Jewish cooking can be described as a "melting pot," with a strong flavor of Eastern Europe, as the majority of Jews in this country are of Ashkenazic (Eastern European) rather than of Sephardic (Mediterranean) background. Hence, Americans generally associate bagels and lox, chicken soup and matzo balls, herring and cheesecake as Jewish food. However, these dishes represent but a small sampling of a very rich and varied tradition of food preparation. Jews from a Sephardic background may never have eaten gefilte fish, latkes or herring, and would be equally surprised to know that many other Jews have never eaten couscous, borekas and mishmishiya.

Just as Jews have always learned to speak the language of the country in which they lived, they learned the regional styles of cooking, adapting as necessary to religious dietary laws of Kashruth that call for the separation of milk and meat, the removal of blood from meat, and the exclusion of shellfish, game birds and pork.

Universally, chicken soup seems to be considered as a panacea, and no doubt dates back to the wonder of that warm, golden broth that would grace the Shabbat table in the Shtetl. Another Shabbat favorite is *cholent*—a slow-cooking casserole dish that cooks overnight on Friday to be eaten hot on Saturday, without having to cook on Shabbat. In the cold of an Eastern European winter, a hot meal on Shabbat was essential. The usual cholent would be made of a little meat and a lot of vegetables. It is interesting to note that in the Yucatán such a dish is prepared on Friday for Saturday, although Judaism is not practiced by the people. A braided bread is also found there!

Jewish food was influenced by the difficult financial circumstances of shtetl life. In fact, from the Middle Ages onward, the majority of Jews lived in ghettoed Europe as the underprivileged poor. Jewish women's ingenuity created varied dishes with the little that was available, which necessitated the development of many dishes that featured stuffed vegetables and soups that would help the little to go a long way. We have thus inherited a variety of recipes for chopped meats or fish. It is interesting to note that during the Middle Ages, Jews were strictly forbidden to buy fish, as it was thought to increase fertility in Jewish males! During the week, shtetl Jews made do with a hunk of unrefined bread and soup or potatoes. This dark bread was replaced on Shabbat with a special white, braided challah, made from white flour, glazed with egg yolk and sprinkled with sesame or poppy seeds, representing the manna in the wilderness.

Chicken, available in the shtetl, was a staple, used first for soup and then eaten as a main course. This was served together with fruit and vegetables, fresh when available, otherwise preserved. Shabbat was the highlight of the week. The sight of the challah sitting between the Shabbat candles and next to the Shabbat wine was an uplifting experience for the family, who would savor foods not possible for them on a daily basis. They worked all week to make Shabbat special.

It can be argued that Judaism has always survived by adapting to modernity. Life has changed drastically in this century and this country. The staff of life from the "old country," in many ways has become the stuff of nostalgia, as our concern for good health overrides our "hamishe" leanings toward our past.

However, it need not be an "either-or" dilemma. Another alternative is to change our way of preparing the old favorites. With this in mind, we have included some low-fat versions of traditional dishes. The cholesterol level of any traditional dish can be lowered by the use of Nyafat (vegetable shortening) or vegetable oil instead of schmaltz (chicken fat), egg substitutes, nonfat sour cream or yogurt, and nonfat cheese, such as cottage cheese, so nonfat cream cheese allows us to have our cheesecake and eat it, too! We recommend that you convert any traditional dish in this manner. These substitutes create great dishes that you will be proud to serve and will fool your guests into thinking that they are eating the "real thing."

In addition to altering the cholesterol level of our cooking, we can take advantage of the fresh produce that surrounds us, particularly in states such as California. Cilantro now graces our Seder plates as the karpas, and an abundant and varied assortment of vegetables has become very popular—for many, replacing meat in their diets. Meat and fish, when prepared, are often broiled, and exotic vegetables are eaten raw.

It may well be that our grandmothers would not feel at home in our kitchens with their modern appliances and alternative ingredients, but we want them to know that we treasure their recipes from the past that link us to them and our history, and help us to span time and to build bridges to our future.

Their recipes are the visual delights, the smells and tastes of past birthdays, Shabbat dinners and Pesach Seders. We want our grandmothers to know that even though we may be too busy or too health-conscious to cook as they did, the saving of their recipes for re-reading and savoring is very important to us and to future generations. We honor our own ethnic cooking, reminding us who we are, and where we have come from.

The robust cuisine of our European past may be too heavy for our climate and for media-dominated stereotypes on a regular basis—this is our inimitable way of adapting. On special occasions, however, we enjoy savoring our traditions of the past— calories and all—and so in keeping with our faith, we end with the traditional injunction, *"Ess mein kindt, ess,"* liberally translated as "Eat, eat my child."

Lorraine Gerstl

What Is Kosher?

Most people know, without a second thought, that observant Jews do not eat pork. But that is only one of the laws of kashrut (permissible foods). As stated in the Bible and elaborated upon in the Talmud and subsequent legal codes, certain animals are permissible to eat; others are forbidden. The Bible defines certain species as "clean" and others as "unclean" (Leviticus 11, Deuteronomy 14:3–21). Today we call permitted foods kosher and forbidden foods treyf.

A kosher animal must be slaughtered and prepared in a ritually correct way—a way that truly is the most humane—in order to remain kosher. And, harking back to the Biblical admonition that "A calf should not be cooked in it's mother's milk," it is forbidden to consume milk and meat within six hours of one another. Thus among observant Jews, separate dishes are used for milk meals and meat meals. Thus chicken (which is kosher) becomes treyf if not slaughtered properly; even if beef is kosher, it can be made treyf by cooking it with dairy products.

Mammals: Those that have split hooves and chew their cuds, the two necessary signs which render them "clean," include cattle, sheep, goats and venison, but Jews may only eat from the front half of these animals. Thus, while chuck and flank are acceptable, sirloin steak, alas, is not. Treyf mammals include pig, rabbit, horse, bear, dog, cat and whale.

Birds and Poultry: The Bible does not stipulate identifying characteristics for birds, but the Mishnah states that "a bird that seizes food in its claws is unclean, while one which has an extra talon, a craw, and a peelable gizzard is clean," (Hulin 3:6). Kosher birds include chicken, duck, goose, pigeon, pheasant, quail and turkey. Birds of prey are all treyf.

Fish: According to the Bible, only fish that have both fins and scales are considered "clean." These include anchovy, bass, bluefish, carp, cod, flounder, fluke, haddock, halibut, herring, mackerel, pike, red snapper, salmon, sardine, shad, sole, trout, tuna and whitefish. Catfish, eel, porpoise and shark may not be eaten. All shellfish are considered treyf. Thus some favorite seafoods such as clams, lobster, oyster, scallops, shrimp, snail, and squid are prohibited. There is a dispute concerning two species of fish because during some parts of their lives they have fins and scales and during others they don't. Orthodox Jews prohibit sturgeon and swordfish. Conservative and Reform Jews permit them.

Finally, although it seems disgusting and hard to believe, locusts, crickets and grasshoppers are considered kosher!

Appetizers

The Sabbath

The importance of the celebration of the Sabbath cannot be underestimated. The Jewish essayist, Ahad Ha-Am once said, "More than the Jewish people have kept the Sabbath, the Sabbath has kept the Jewish people." Sabbath, the weekly celebration of God's gift to us, is celebrated both in communal worship and at the home through what might have been the one good meal of the week and the chance to relax, enjoy one's family and sing praises to God.

The family has been the means through which traditional Jewish celebrations have survived and flourished. And as the family has preserved those celebrations through the ages, today these observances can greatly enhance and unify the family.

The Sabbath is the most important of our holidays, and it is the only one mentioned in the Ten Commandments. This may be the reason for its importance, as well as the opportunity for connecting to God every week in this special way.

Traditionally, the weekly day of rest gives family members the time together away from ordinary everyday activities. That separation and togetherness has never been more needed than in these days of our fast-paced life. During the week each member of the family is busy doing their own thing. The Sabbath day provides the time to be together—time to talk and worship.

It begins on Friday evening by lighting and blessing at least two candles, symbolizing their bringing light and consciousness into our lives.

The wine is blessed, reminding us of the sweetness of life, and challah, the egg-rich, braided bread, is reserved as a special treat for Shabbat. Poor families would have saved and scrimped all week long for the Sabbath evening meal. Traditionally, chicken was boiled to make a soup and then the meat became the main course. The uniquely Jewish cholent, a Jewish casserole, is an ancient dish going back to Biblical times and is traditionally served on Saturday afternoon, a day when no cooking is permitted. The dish would be put into the oven before sundown on Friday evening and left to cook slowly overnight, served warm and tasty.

In the winter, a warm meal was essential. In the days before households had individual stoves, the dish would be brought to the community baker and returned for the Saturday meal. The main ingredients are potatoes, beans, onions and a little meat. Now we recognize the energy and health value of small amounts of meat and the positive value of legumes.

Chopped Liver

Fry onions until well browned. Add liver to onions and fry until liver is no longer pink. Remove from pan.

Chop liver, onions and 4 eggs together in food processor. Chop apple very fine and add to liver. Salt and pepper to taste.

Mound on platter, sprinkle with finely chopped egg white and egg yolk and garnish with parsley.

5 Tbsps. vegetable oil
1 large onion
1 lb. chicken or calf's liver
4 hard-boiled eggs
1 small green apple, peeled
  Salt and pepper
1 hard-boiled egg and parsley to decorate

★

Traditional Chopped Herring

32 oz. wine herring snacks
(available in any
grocery store)
2½ apples, peeled and
cored (you may use red
and/or green)
5 eggs, hard boiled
1 large onion
2 Tbsps. sugar
2 pieces of matzo

For decoration:
3 eggs, hard boiled
Parsley, a few sprigs
Red pepper, small
amount, sliced
Capers
Olives

Remove bay leaves and peppercorns from the jars of herring. In a food processor, process herring, apples, eggs and onions. Add sugar and matzo for a few seconds. Mound the mixture on a plate (traditionally in the shape of a fish). To decorate: Chop the whites and yolks of the eggs separately. Sprinkle all ingredients over the top of the herring mixture.

Gefilte Fish

Put fish and 2 onions through grinder using, fine blade or food processor, being careful not to over-process. Put in bowl. Stir in eggs, salt, pepper and sugar. Mix while adding about ½ cup water to make a soft mixture. Stir in matzo meal and mix thoroughly.

In a large kettle, place fish heads, bones and skin. Add 2 quarts cold water, 1 tsp. salt, ¼ tsp. white pepper and 1 tsp. sugar. Bring to boil. Simmer for 30 minutes. Remove from heat. Remove fish heads and bones from the kettle.

Wet hands and form balls out of the fish mixture and place in the kettle. Add whole onion and sliced carrots. There should be enough liquid to cover the fish. If not, add water.

Cover kettle, bring to a boil, uncover, reduce heat and simmer for 2½ hours until stock is less than half. Carefully remove fish balls to a serving platter.

Strain fish stock and pour some over the fish. Arrange carrots and parsley around platter as a garnish. Cool and refrigerate until stock jells. Serve with horseradish.

3 lbs. fish (2 lbs. fat fish, 1 lb. lean fish; whitefish and pike are always good choices) with head, bones and skin removed but reserved
3 medium onions
3 eggs, well beaten
2 tsps. salt
¼ tsp. white pepper
1 tsp. sugar
3 Tbsps. matzo meal
3 carrots, sliced in rounds
Parsley for decoration

What Is Gefilte Fish?

Gefilte fish—stuffed fish—is a concept that may date back to the Middle Ages. In the eighteenth century in Eastern Europe, Gefilte fish was often a forcemeat made from chopped freshwater fish and matzo crumbs that was stuffed into slices of carp. Or it could be a whole carp stuffed with its own chopped flesh and flavorings and baked or poached. Today it is usually prepared as plain chopped fish balls, not encased in a skin. Eating fish at the Friday Sabbath meal has been traditional since the Talmudic Era.

Pickled Herring

3 medium or 2 large
cleaned and prepared
herring, with skin
1 large onion, sliced thin
1 cup vinegar
¼ cup water
1 Tbsp. brown sugar
3 bay leaves
1 tsp. mixed whole spice
(optional)
12 peppercorns
6 thin slices of lemon,
seeds removed
2 Tbsps. sour cream
(optional)

Cut herring into 1" square cubes and place them in a quart jar. Add onion. Bring vinegar, water and sugar to a quick boil and cool until lukewarm. Add liquid to jar with bay leaves, spices and lemon slices. Stir in sour cream, if desired. Cover and let stand 24 hours before serving.

★

Sweet and Sour Salmon

Combine the onions, lemon slices, brown sugar, raisins, bay leaf, salmon steaks, salt and water in a saucepan. Cover and cook over low heat for 25 minutes. Transfer to a large serving dish. Add the gingersnaps, vinegar and almonds to the fish stock. Cook over low heat, stirring occasionally until smooth. Pour over the fish. Serve warm or cold. Serves 6.

- 2 onions, thinly sliced
- 2 lemons, sliced
- ⅓ cup brown sugar
- ¼ cup seedless white raisins
- 1 bay leaf
- 6 salmon steaks
- 2 tsp. salt
- 2 cups water
- 6 gingersnaps, crushed
- ⅓ cup cider vinegar
- ¼ cup sliced blanched almonds

☆

Mushroom Piroshke

8 oz. cream cheese
½ cup butter, room
    temperature
1½ cups flour

Filling:
3 Tbsps. butter
1 onion, finely chopped
½ lb. mushrooms, finely
    chopped
¼ tsp. thyme
½ tsp. salt
    Pepper, to taste
2 Tbsps. flour
¼ cup sweet or sour
    cream

ix cream cheese and ½ cup butter until smooth. Add flour and work with fingers or pastry blender until smooth. (Or process all ingredients at once in food processor until dough forms a ball. Chill at least 30 minutes.

In sauté pan, heat remaining butter and lightly brown onions. Add mushrooms and cook about 3 minutes, stirring often. Add thyme, salt and pepper and sprinkle with flour. Stir in cream and cook gently until thickened.

Preheat oven to 400°. Roll out dough to ⅛" thickness on a floured cloth or board. Cut into 3" rounds. Place ½ to 1 tsp. filling in center, fold over in half and crimp edges with a fork. Piroshkes can be frozen at this point. Prick top crust. Place on ungreased baking sheet and bake until brown, about 15 minutes.

Sabbath Salmon Spread

Blend first three ingredients together. Mix in onion. Cover and refrigerate overnight. Spread on warm bagels or challah.

6½ oz. smoked salmon, flaked
8 oz. pkg cream cheese
1½ tsp. horseradish
⅓ onion, chopped fine

☆

Hummus

2½ cups canned chickpeas, drained
3 Tbsps. light sesame oil or olive oil
4 Tbsps. lemon juice
2 cloves garlic, crushed
½ tsp. salt
Paprika
Parsley as garnish

Put all ingredients into a blender and purée until smooth. Refrigerate for 8 hours before serving. Sprinkle with paprika and parsley. Makes 4 servings.

Soups and Salads

Rosh Hashanah

According to tradition, Rosh Hashanah is the anniversary of creation, or, in other words, the birthday of the human race. Jewish New Year provides us the opportunity to take stock of our relations with others and make changes and to begin to renew our spiritual selves. We begin the year among our family and close friends.

Everything one does is written down in the Book of Life. On Rosh Hasahanah, those deeds are examined in Heaven. The good and bad deeds of the previous year are weighed and judged. "On Rosh Hashanah it is written and on Yom Kippur it is sealed...who shall live and who shall die...but repentance, prayer and charity temper Judgment's severe decree." The traditional Rosh Hashanah greeting, "May you be inscribed for a good year," has a particularly deep meaning.

Apples, traditionally a symbol of fertility, are dipped in honey to insure a "sweet year," and a challah in a round form, as a symbol of life without end, are traditionally served.

Yom Kippur

Yom Kippur is observed rather than celebrated. This Holy Day, the most solemn of the Jewish Year, ends the ten day penitential period that begins with Rosh Hashanah. It is during these ten days that Jews reflect on their past wrongs. It is said, "Forgiveness is not given until asked for from those you might have harmed." Synagogue prayers are in the plural. No one is exempt, as the congregation prays for absolution for sins committed "knowingly or unknowingly." It is considered the most important day of the calendar even by those who observe seldom or at no other time.

Traditionally, Yom Kippur is a day of fasting. No cooking or eating is done. With the final sounding of the shofar, the ram's horn, the end of the day of prayer is announced, and the twenty-four hour fast is customarily broken by eating something sweet, symbol of a sweet year to come.

Beet Borscht

Cover beets with water and boil until tender. Remove beets from pot and strain liquid into soup pot. Slip beet skins off and grate beets on fine grater into the beet juice (which has been strained). Add 1 Tbsp. salt and 4 cups of boiling water. Bring to quick boil, reduce heat and cook for 5 minutes. Add vinegar and sweeten to taste. Cool and chill in closed jars. Add 1 or 2 Tbsps. sour cream and a boiled potato to each plateful just before serving.

8 small beets
4 cups boiling water
  Salt, to taste
½ cup mild vinegar or
¼ cup lemon juice or
¼ tsp. citric acid crystals
½ to 1 cup sugar, to taste

What is Borscht?

The name Borscht comes from a Russian word meaning cow parsnips. For Russian, Lithuanian and Polish Jews, beet roots (Borscht), cabbage (sauerkraut) and spinach or sorrel (schav) made up a category of foods known as "sours." Their flavors counterbalance the dull taste of the black bread and potatoes that were mainstays of the daily diet.

☆

Spinach Borscht (Schav)

10 oz. frozen chopped
   spinach
 6 cups cold water
 2 tsp. salt or to taste
 1 bunch green onions,
   finely sliced (incl. white
   portion)
   Lemon juice, to taste
 8 oz. cucumber, peeled
   and diced
 8 oz. sour cream or plain
   yogurt

Place frozen spinach in a kettle with water and salt. Cook on low heat until spinach is thawed. Separate the spinach, then turn up the heat and bring to a boil. Turn heat to low and simmer for 7 minutes. Remove from stove and cool completely.

Add salt, sliced green onions and lemon juice to taste. Refrigerate until ready to eat. Serve borscht well chilled, mixed with diced cucumber and topped with a dollop of sour cream or yogurt.

Beef Borscht

Fry onions. Season with salt and pepper. Add carrots and celery and cover with water. Cook until vegetables are soft. Add cabbage and beets and their juice. Add sugar and lemon juice to taste, dill weed, and more salt if necessary. Add potatoes and meat balls about 1 hour before the soup is to be served. Sprinkle dill weed on top

1 lb. ground beef with a little salt and pepper, shaped into small balls
2–3 large onions, chopped
   salt and pepper to taste
2 carrots, cut into rounds
1 bunch celery
1 medium-sized cabbage, thinly sliced
5–6 cans whole beets (julienne)
   Sugar to taste
1 Tbsp. lemon juice
   Dill weed to taste
4–5 boiling potatoes, diced

☆

Orthodox? Conservative? Reform? Chabad?

Although there are several "classifications" of Jews based on their own philosophies of ritual observance, for the most part Jews recognize the following major movements:

Orthodox: Orthodox Jews are strict constructionists of the Bible. They will not eat any but strictly Kosher foods; they use separate plates and cutlery for milk and meat products. Men and women sit in separate sections of the House of Worship—and never together. When a Jewish girl marries, she shaves her head (or cuts her hair very short) and wears a wig in public (lest any man but her husband sees her natural hair, which is considered sensual and thus taboo). Men and women do not dance together and do not touch one another or display any type of tactile affection unless they are married, and even then they usually touch only in private.

Israel recognizes only Orthodox Rabbis as Rabbis. In Israel, the only marriage ceremony recognized is performed by an Orthodox Rabbi under strictly Orthodox conditions. That is why a large proportion of Israeli Jews have their weddings performed on the nearby island of Cyprus. In Orthodox Judaism, the liturgy is read only in Hebrew or Aramaic. Ritual prayer, both at home and outside the home, is rigorously observed.

Conservative: The Conservative movement subscribes to a more liberal philosophy than Orthodox. The laws of *kashruth* (Kosher) usually are observed to a degree, but failure to observe all of the rules is not critical—this is an individual preference. The liturgy is generally read in Hebrew. Jewish males always wear *kipot* or *yarmulkes* (skullcaps) and usually wear a *tallit* (prayer shawl) when praying in the Synagogue. Israelis do not recognize Conservative or Reform Rabbis as Rabbis.

Reform: Numerically the largest number of Jews in the United States, Reform Judaism represents the most liberal of the major Jewish movements. A *yarmulke* is optional in the Synagogue, although in some Houses of Worship it is not worn. The liturgy is predominantly in English (or the language of the country) with some Hebrew thrown in. In a large number of congregations, God is now gender neutral, and the new Prayer Book is so written. Feminists find a home within the movement, as do Gays and Lesbians. On the other hand, Orthodox Jews (and a number of Conservatives as well) find Reform Judaism to be anathema—a Reform Jew is not seen as a real Jew.

Chabad: A hyperaggressive, militant offshoot of Orthodox Judaism, Chabad traces its roots directly to that movement of Eighteenth Century Eastern European Hasidic Jews known as the *Lubavitchers* (from a community in Southern Poland). Unlike most Jewish movements, Chabad actively proselytizes—but among Jews themselves, rather than Christians. Controversial though Chabad may be, they have unquestionably raised the level of Jewish identity wherever they put down roots.

Chicken Soup

P lace washed chicken, including extra backs and necks, in a large pot and cover with water. Bring to a fast boil and skim off the scum that rises to the top. Place whole onion, celery, carrots and salt and pepper in the soup. Simmer for 1 hour. Add whole sprigs of parsley. Simmer for 1 more hour. Strain soup through a sieve and chill to congeal fat on top. Before serving, remove fat and heat.

1 whole chicken, cut up, with extra backs and necks
1 large onion
3 stalks celery, with leaves
4 carrots
Salt and pepper, to taste
Fresh parsley, to taste

☆

Ettie's Baked Knaidelach

3 matzos
3 onions, chopped
  Vegetable oil
3 eggs, beaten
3 Tbsps. Nyafat vegetable
  shortening (or
  schmaltz)
3 Tbsps. water
3 Tbsps. matzo meal
  Salt, pepper, cinnamon
  and ginger to taste

 oak matzos in water until soft. Squeeze semi-dry. Fry onions in vegetable oil. Add matzo, eggs, shortening, water and matzo meal. Add spices.

Remove mixture from heat and knead into small balls.

Preheat oiled roasting pan in 350° oven. Place balls in pan and roast at 350° until brown. Remove.

Knaidelach may be added to soup or eaten dry as an accompaniment to soup.

What Are Knaidelach?

Knaidelach is the Yiddish word for dumplings. In the winter, big dumplings were made from potato dough and were often filled with oatmeal, chopped onions and goose or chicken fat. Smaller, more digestible dumplings, were made from mashed potatoes that were placed in a bowl of warm milk. Today, Knaidelach are made from matzo meal and are served in chicken soup at Passover and the year around.

Kreplach

Mix flour and salt. Add eggs and water. Stir or knead until you have a smooth dough. Set aside for 1 hour at room temperature in a plastic bag.

Melt schmaltz in a skillet. Add onions. Sauté until translucent. Add beef. Cook mixture until meat is no longer pink. Remove from heat. Add parsley, salt and pepper.

After dough has rested for 1 hour, divide it in half. Set half the dough aside in a plastic bag. Roll the other half of the dough until almost paper thin.

Cut the finished sheet into 2½" squares. Use the scraps of dough that are left over to add to the rest of the dough and make more squares.

To fill the kreplach, use 1 tsp. of filling for each square. Place the filling in the center and fold over diagonally to make a triangle. Press the ends firmly to seal. Then bend each triangular krepl around your finger and press the two ends of the triangle together. As you make the kreplach, set them out in neat rows on a clean, dry kitchen cloth.

Repeat this process until all the dough and all the filling are used up. The recipe makes between 18 and 20 kreplach.

Bring 4 quarts of salted water to a rapid boil. Gently drop the kreplach into the pot and cook for 20–25 minutes. Remove the kreplach with a slotted spoon. Drain.

While the kreplach are cooking, heat 2 quarts of chicken stock in another pot. Mix ½ cup of finely chopped parsley and chives together. After the kreplach are cooked, put two or three in each soup bowl and ladle the soup over them. Sprinkle each portion of the soup with the herbs and serve. Serves 6–8 people.

Dough:
- 2 cups white flour
  Pinch of salt
- 2 large eggs
- 4 tsps. cold water (more, if needed)

Filling:
- 1 Tbsp. schmaltz (chicken fat) (or Nyafat vegetable shortening)
- ½ cup onions, very finely chopped
- ½ lb. lean ground beef
- 1 tsp. fresh chopped parsley
  Salt and pepper to taste
- 2 qts. chicken stock
- ½ cup parsley or chives, finely chopped

☆

Russian Mushroom-Barley Soup

3 quarts water

1½ lbs. stew meat, cubed
   (plus bones, optional,
   see below)

3 carrots, scrubbed

5 stalks celery

2 medium onions,
   quartered

1½ cups mushrooms,
   sliced, or ¾ cup dried
   mushrooms

1½ cups pearl barley

Boil the stew meat in salted water (some knuckle bones or marrow-filled soup bones make a nice addition). Skim the fat. Slice carrots and celery into large chunks and add to the boiling stock. Add onions, mushrooms and barley. Season to taste with salt and pepper. Simmer over low heat. If too thick when barley has finished absorbing liquid, add more water. Serve with rye bread. (It's even better the next day, for reasons known only to the Divine One and the Russian Jews).

☆

Eggplant Salad

Cut unpeeled eggplant into small cubes. In a large skillet, heat ½ cup olive oil over moderately high heat. Sauté eggplant, turning and stirring until nicely browned, about 10 minutes. Add onion, celery and green pepper. Cook and stir until vegetables are crisp-tender, adding more oil, if necessary. Stir in tomato purée, olives, vinegar, sugar and salt. Simmer uncovered for 10 minutes, stirring occasionally. Remove from heat. Cool and refrigerate several hours or overnight. May be refrigerated up to 1 week or frozen. Makes 4 cups.

- 1 large eggplant
- ½ to ¾ cup olive oil
- 1 cup chopped onion
- 1 cup chopped celery
- 1 cup chopped green pepper
- 1 cup tomato purée (8 oz)
- ½ cup chopped black olives
- ⅓ cup red wine vinegar
- 2 Tbsps. sugar
- 1½ tsp. salt

Funny, You Don't Sound Jewish....

As a fun bit of trivia, here are the names of some famous Jewish personalities who "altered" their original names a bit. Their real names appear in parentheses:

Edie Adams (Elizabeth Edith Enke)

Joey Adams (Joseph Abramowitz)

Mel Allen (Melvin Israel)

Woody Allen (Allen Konigsberg)

Beatrice Arthur (Bernice Frankel)

Lauren Bacall (Betty Joan Perske)

Theda Bara (Theodosia Goodman)

Rona Barrett (Rona Burstein)

Robbie Benson (Robert Segal)

Milton Berle (Milton Berlinger)

Jack Benny (Benjamin Kubelsky)

Joey Bishop (Joseph Gottlieb)

Victor Borge (Borge Rosenbaum)

Fanny Brice (Fanny Borach)

Albert Brooks (Albert Einstein)

Mel Brooks (Melvin Kaminsky)

Lenny Bruce (Leonard Alfred Schneider)

George Burns (Nathan Birnbaum)

Dyan Cannon (Samile Diane Friesen)

Eddie Cantor (Isidor Iskowitch)

Al Capp (Alfred Gerald Caplin)

Kitty Carlisle (Catherine Holzman)

Jeff Chandler (Ira Grossel)

Cyd Charisse (Tula Finklea)

Lee J. Cobb (Leo Jacoby)

David Copperfield (David Kotkin)

Howard Cosell (Howard Cohen)

Alan King (Irwin Kniberg)

Carole King (Carole Klein)

Larry King (Larry Zeigler)

Bert Lahr (Irving Lahrheim)

Michael Landon (Eugene Orowitz)

Steve Lawrence (Sidney Leibowitz)

Michelle Lee (Michelle Dusiak)

Pinky Lee (Pincus Leff)

Jerry Lewis (Joseph Levitch)

Hal Linden (Harold Lipshitz)

Peter Lorre (Laszlo Lowenstein)

Fredric March (Fredrick Bickel)

Tony Martin (Alvin Morris)

Golda Meir (Goldie Meyerson)

Ethel Merman (Ethel Zimmerman)

David Merrick (David Margulies)

Yves Montand (Ivo Levi)

Paul Muni (Muni Weisenfreund)

Arthur Murray (Arthur Teichman)

Mike Nichols (Michael Peschlowsky)

Bert Parks (Bert Jacobson)

Jan Peerce (Jacob Perelmuth)

Tony Randall (Leonard Rosenberg)

Joan Rivers (Joan Molinsky)

Harold Robbins (Harold Rubin)

Edward G. Robinson (Emmanuel Goldenberg)

Billy Rose (William Rosenberg)

Maybe It's the Food.

Tony Curtis (Bernard Schwartz)

Howard DaSilva (Howard Silverblatt)

Rodney Dangerfield (Jacob Cohen)

Phyllis Diller (Phyllis Driver)

Kirk Douglas (Issur Danielovitch Demsky)

Melvyn Douglas (Melvyn Hesselberg)

Michael Douglas (Michael Demsky)

Bob Dylan (Robert Zimmerman)

John Forsythe (John Freund)

John Garfield (Julius Garfinkle)

Lee Grant (Lyova Rosenthal)

Joel Gray (Joe Katz)

Buddy Hackett (Leonard Hacker)

Barbara Hershey (Barbara Herzstine)

Harry Houdini (Erich Weiss)

Leslie Howard (Leslie Stainer)

David Janssen (David Meyer)

Danny Kaye (David Kaminsky)

Winona Ryder (Winona Horowitz)

Mort Sahl (Morton Lyon)

Susan St. James (Susan Miller)

Jill St. John (Jill Oppenheim)

Soupy Sales (Milton Hines)

Jane Seymour (Joyce Frankenberg)

Artie Shaw (Arthur Arshansky)

Dick Shawn (Richard Schuler)

Dinah Shore (Frances Rose Shore)

Beverly Sills (Belle Silverman)

Irving Stone (Irving Tennenbaum)

Mike Todd (Avrom Girsch Goldbogen)

Sophie Tucker (Sonia Kalish)

Mike Wallace (Mike Wallach)

Nathaniel West (Nathan Weinstein)

Gene Wilder (Jerome Silberman)

Shelley Winters (Shirley Schrift)

Turkish Shepherd's Salad

4 tomatoes, chopped
2 medium onions, chopped
1 green pepper, chopped
1 cucumber, sliced, then chopped
1 small bunch parsley, chopped fine
1–3 mint leaves, chopped fine
Lemon juice to taste
Sugar to taste

 Mix vegetables together. Add sugar (1 tsp.–1 Tbsp., to taste) and pour lemon juice over the salad. Mix well and serve.

☆

Tabbouleh (Cracked Wheat Salad)

Rinse bulgur wheat under cold water; drain well. Turn into a large bowl. Cover with boiling water. Let bulgur soak 1–2 hours. Drain; squeeze out excess moisture with your hands.

Dressing: In a medium bowl, combine olive oil, lemon juice, garlic, salt and pepper. Mix well.

Add bulgur to dressing. Toss lightly to mix well. Turn into a large glass bowl. Mix all ingredients and refrigerate, tightly covered, overnight.

Serves 10 to 12.

1 cup cracked bulgur wheat

Dressing:
- ¾ cup olive oil or salad oil
- 3 Tbsps. lemon juice
- 1 clove garlic, crushed
- 1½ tsps. salt
- ½ tsp. pepper
- ¾ cup scallions, finely chopped
- 1 cup cucumbers, pared and cut into ¼" cubes
- 1½ cups parsley, finely chopped
- ¾ cup fresh mint, finely chopped
- 4 medium tomatoes, peeled and cut into ½" cubes
  Fresh mint sprigs

★

Dairy, Grains, and Noodles

Sukkot

Every symbol and message of Sukkot cooperates to make the Jew conscious of nature and the world in which we live. Steeped in the agricultural origins of the people of Biblical times, Sukkot also commemorates God's watchful care over the Israelites as they dwelt in fragile huts during the forty years of wandering in the desert wilderness before they entered the promised land. Sukkot is the ancestor of our American Thanksgiving. We give thanks for the blessing of the harvest and for God's miraculous production through the ages.

The holiday begins with the construction of a Sukkah, a temporary arbor out in the garden or open space, followed by eight celebratory days of meals shared in the Sukkah. The Sukkah is decorated with cornstalks, gourds, pumpkins and children's pictures.

The lulav, a palm branch combined with myrtle and willow branches tied together, and the etrog, a lemon-like citron, are the four festival symbols that may have been ancient talismans for rain, and represent different facets of the human body: the palm representing the spine; the willow, the eyes; the myrtle, the lips; and the etrog, the human heart.

Simchat Torah

Simchat Torah celebrates the completion of the yearly cycle of Torah readings, culminating in reading the last chapters of Deuteronomy and immediately starting the reading of the first chapter of Genesis. The process of continuity of endings and beginnings is symbolized by the seven ceremonial processional circuits of congregants carrying as many Torahs and replicas as available. The Simchat Torah procession originated in the 16th century as a way of enabling children to feel closer to the Torah. Folklorists say that ceremonial circling was one of the oldest ways in which man used to try to appease the spirits; evil ones were thought to be kept out of the circle. It is customary to eat round foods to symbolize the wholeness of the year. Today Israeli flags topped with apples are added to the procession.

Ettie's Cheese Blintzes

Batter:
- **6 eggs, beaten well**
- **1 tsp. salt**
- **6 Tbsps. vegetable or peanut oil**
- **3 cups flour**
- **3–3½ cups water**

Filling:
- **1 pint cottage cheese**
- **2 heaping Tbsps. sugar**
- **2 egg yolks**
- **2 level Tbsps. sifted flour**
- **Pinch cinnamon**
- **Pinch salt**

 Blend beaten eggs and salt. Add oil slowly. Alternately add flour and water. Let the mixture sit for 20 minutes in refrigerator.

Heat lightly oiled pan. A non-stick, Teflon-coated pan is the perfect cooking utensil. Pour in small amount of batter. Remove from heat and swirl the batter around to thinly coat the pan. Pour off any excess batter (which may be re-used).

Sauté the batter on one side only. Let the blintz cook until it looks as if it is almost totally cooked through, then remove it onto a dish or other flat surface. The bottom of the blintz should be light and barely beginning to brown around the edges. Repeat this procedure until all the batter is used up.

Mash the cheese and mix everything else into it to make the filling. Place a heaping Tbsp. of filling onto one side of the blintz. Spread it over the length of the blintz, leaving ¼" margin on both ends. Fold lengthwise side of the blintz that is closest to you over the filling. Fold the two shorter, perpendicular ends of the blintz across this fold. Then roll up the blintz jelly roll fashion. The result will be a short, cylindrical, cigar-shape. Repeat this step until all the filling and all the blintzes are used up. You may or may not have filling left over. Do not exceed 1 Tbsp. of filling per blintz or the blintzes may burst during cooking.

Preheat oven to 450°. Arrange the filled and rolled blintzes in a well-buttered baking dish. Dot with bits of sweet butter. Bake the blintzes for 10 to 15 minutes and serve immediately.

Serving suggestion: When serving blintzes as a dessert, accompany them with sour cream and a seasonal fruit compote.

What Are Blintzes?

Blintzes are filled pancakes related to the Ukrainian blinchiki and the Russian blini. Blintzes were an everyday food of Central and Eastern European Jews, although the use of wheat flour and eggs meant that they were enjoyed more often by the well-to-do. In the United States today, Blintzes are paper-thin pancakes made from a wheat flour and egg batter, folded up like a Chinese egg roll around a filling. Cheese is the most common filling. Blintzes are fried golden brown on both sides.

Blintz Soufflé

I n a medium bowl or food processor fitted with a metal blade, combine all filling ingredients until blended.

Preheat oven to 350°. Butter a 9×13" baking dish; set aside. In a blender, mix margarine, sugar, eggs, sour cream, orange juice, flour and baking powder until blended.

Pour half of the batter into a prepared baking dish. Drop filling by heaped spoonfuls over batter. Spread evenly with a knife. It will mix with the batter.

Pour remaining batter over filling. Unbaked soufflé may be covered and refrigerated several hours or overnight until ready to use.

Before baking, bring soufflé to room temperature. Bake, uncovered, 50–60 minutes or until puffed and golden. Serve immediately with sour cream and a blueberry syrup or assorted jams.

Makes 8 servings.

¼ lb. margarine, softened
⅓ cup sugar
6 eggs
1½ cups dairy sour cream
½ cup orange juice
1 cup all-purpose flour
2 tsps. baking powder

Blintz filling:
1 (8 oz.) pkg. cream cheese, cut up
2 cups small curd cottage cheese
2 egg yolks
1 Tbsp. sugar
1 tsp. vanilla extract

☆

Kasha Varnishkes

3 Tbsps. olive or
   vegetable oil
2 medium onions, sliced
½ lb. fresh mushrooms
1 cup cooked kasha
   (buckwheat groats)
2 cups cooked bow tie
   noodles
   Salt and pepper to taste

auté onions and mushrooms in olive oil until soft. Add kasha and bow ties and heat in skillet to blend flavors. Season. Can be made a day or two in advance and reheated in oven.

What is Kasha?

Kasha is the Russian name for buckwheat groats. In the past, it was consumed so frequently that there arose a saying among the Russians that "Buckwheat gruel is our mother and rye bread is our father."

Orange Couscous Pilaf

Bring orange juice, water, salt, margarine or butter and currants to a boil in a covered kettle. Remove from heat. Stir in dry couscous. Cover and let stand 15 minutes, then fluff with a fork. Reheat if necessary and stir in the almonds just before serving.

Makes 4 cups of pilaf.

1 cup orange juice
½ cup water
½ tsp. salt
1 Tbsp. margarine or butter
2 oz. dried currants
1 cup dry couscous grains
1 oz. sliced almonds

☆

Couscous Pilaf

2 cups boiling water, chicken or vegetable stock
1 cup couscous
½ tsp. salt
2 Tbsps. olive oil
1 large onion, chopped
2 scallions, chopped
1 red bell pepper, chopped
1 zucchini, chopped
½ cup cooked chickpeas
½ cup golden raisins
¼ cup parsley, chopped
Crushed red pepper, to taste

ombine water or broth, salt and couscous and cover until all the liquid is absorbed (about 5 minutes). In a large skillet, heat oil. Add onion, scallions, bell pepper and zucchini and cook over medium heat until soft. Place in an oven-proof casserole dish and add remaining ingredients. Dot with margarine and bake for 20 minutes in a 350° oven.

★

Lukshen Kugel

Grate apples into large mixing bowl. Add eggs and beat. Add vanilla, orange juice, raisins, sugar, cinnamon and orange rind. Mix well. Cook noodles according to package instructions and drain well. Add noodles to above mixture and gently stir to mix. Pour kugel mixture into two 9×13″ pans and dot with butter. Bake at 350° on bottom oven shelf for 45–55 minutes.

1½ **green apples or cooking apples**
6 **large eggs**
3 **tsps. vanilla**
¾ **cup orange juice**
¾ **cup seedless raisins**
1 **cup sugar**
2½ **Tbsps. ground cinnamon or to taste**
2–3 **Tbsps. grated orange rind**
20 **oz. wide noodles**
8–12 **Tbsps. unsalted butter**

What is Kugel?

Kugel—pudding—was a customary food on the Sabbath. Along with cholent, the kugel would be taken on Friday to a baker, who often was not Jewish, and collected the next day. The taking and collecting, which might be accomplished by the married women or by young unmarried men and women, was part of the social ritual of the community, serving as an opportunity for gossip or as a sort of youth club and marriage bureau. Today, kugels are often made with noodles, dried fruits and eggs.

Vegetables & Potatoes

Chanukah

Chanukah, also spelled Hanukkah, the festival of rededication, is an eight-day festival occurring during the month of December. It commemorates the rededication of the Second Temple in 165 B.C.E., when, against all odds, a small group of Jews overcame the mighty Syrian oppressors, who sought to obliterate Jewish belief and convert all Jews to the way of Hellenism. More important, it was the very first time in history when a people fought successfully to win freedom of religion for all peoples. When the victory was achieved, the immediate concern was to purify the Temple and reconsecrate the altar for the renewal of daily services.

The lovely story, if not necessarily based on traceable fact, is that when the Jews were cleansing the Temple, only one undefiled vial of oil for burning in the everlasting light could be found. Through a miracle, this one bottle of oil lasted not only for one day, but for eight days—enough time to allow the Jews to process new, undefiled oil. In commemoration of this miracle, the festival is celebrated for eight days. Lights are burned in a special eight-branched Menorah, beginning with one light and adding one each night. Chanukah is a festival primarily celebrated in the home, with the lighting and blessing of the Menorah candles and the eating of foods cooked in oil, such as latkes. Some say it takes a whole year to recover from the cholesterol overload! The playing of a game with a spinning top called the Dreidel, singing, children's plays and the giving of gifts are all part of the holiday. It is not—and never has been—the "Jewish Christmas."

Tirtsa's Carrots

3 or 4 carrots
1 Tbsp. butter or
margarine
½ tsp. cumin
1 tsp. sugar
1 clove garlic, mashed or
minced
Salt and pepper

eel, slice and boil carrots until tender. Drain and set aside. Melt butter or margarine in pan and add cumin, sugar and garlic. Sauté a minute and return carrots to pan, tossing to coat with sauce. Season to taste.

★

Carrot Ring

ix above (egg yolks only). Fold in egg whites. Bake in greased ring or loaf pan at 350° for 40 minutes.

½ cup brown sugar
1 cup corn oil
2 eggs, separated, whites beaten
1 cup grated carrots
1¼ cups flour
½ tsp. baking powder
½ tsp. baking soda
    Pinch of salt (optional)
2 Tbsps. water

★

Bulgur Stuffed Squash

½ cup shredded carrot
½ cup chopped onion
2 Tbsps. butter or margarine
1 10½ oz. can condensed chicken broth
1 cup water
1 cup bulgur wheat
1 Tbsp. dried parsley flakes
½ tsp. dried oregano, crushed
¼ tsp. salt
⅛ tsp. pepper
⅓ cup chopped walnuts
1 3½–4 lb. butternut or acorn squash

I n a saucepan, cook shredded carrot and chopped onion in butter or margarine until tender. Stir in condensed chicken broth, water, bulgur wheat, parsley flakes, oregano, salt and ⅛ tsp pepper. Bring to a boil. Cover and reduce heat. Simmer for 15 minutes. Stir in chopped walnuts.

Meanwhile, cut top off squash. Remove seeds. Season inside of squash generously with salt and pepper.

Turn the bulgur mixture into the squash cavity. Cover tightly with foil. Bake in a 375° oven for 1–1¼ hours or until squash is tender. Makes 6–8 servings.

Beverly's Potatoes

Spray Pyrex dish with Pam or other nonstick spray. Layer potatoes in dish. Sprinkle salt, pepper, garlic salt and Italian herbs onto potatoes. Drizzle a small amount of olive oil onto the potatoes. Bake at 350° for 1 hour.

7 potatoes, unpeeled,
  sliced into ¼" rounds
  Salt, to taste
  Black pepper, to taste
  Garlic salt, to taste
2 Tbsps. Italian herbs
  Small amount of
  olive oil

☆

Sweet & Sour Red Cabbage

1 Tbsp. butter or margarine

½ cup wine vinegar

¼ cup honey

1 tsp. salt

1 medium head (8 cups) red cabbage, shredded

2 apples, cored and diced

elt butter in large non-stick skillet over medium heat. Stir in vinegar, honey and salt. Add cabbage and apples; toss well. Reduce heat to low; cover and simmer 45–50 minutes.

To microwave: Place shredded cabbage in 3 quart microwave safe baking dish. Add apples, butter and vinegar. Cover and cook on high for 15 minutes. Stir in honey and salt. Cover and cook on high for an additional 10 minutes.

Berenjena (Israeli Fried Eggplant)

Soak eggplant in salted water. Drain well and dry slices. Dip in seasoned flour, then into beaten eggs. Brown well on each side in preheated oil. Drain well on paper towels. Place slices in sauce in baking pan in 350° oven for 30 minutes.

1 eggplant, large, peeled and sliced
½ tsp. salt
  Pepper, to taste
½ cup flour
1–2 eggs, beaten
  Oil for frying

Sauce:
  ½ cup tomato sauce
  ½ cup water
  ½ tsp. sugar
  1 clove garlic, chopped

☆

Potato Latkes

4 large potatoes (or 6
 medium potatoes)
1 small onion
2 eggs
1 Tbsp. flour or matzo
 meal
½ tsp. salt
 Dash pepper
 Vegetable oil for frying

Grate potatoes with onion by hand or blender, either coarse or fine. Drain excess water. Add eggs, flour, salt and pepper. Mix well. Heat frying pan or electric fryer with a layer of oil. Drop large spoonfuls into the frying pan or electric fryer. Don't make the latkes too thick—they must fry all the way through. Turn when the latkes are golden brown. Drain on paper towel before serving. Serve with applesauce, sugar, cinnamon and/or sour cream.

What Are Latkes?

Latkes are potato pancakes, a common food of Lithuanian Jews, who made them from grated potatoes fried in poppyseed oil or fat. Jews in the Ukraine and other Eastern European regions were accustomed to eating buckwheat latkes instead. Fried latkes are popular at Chanukah because of the association of fried foods with the miracle of the oil.

Aunt Dorothy's Mashed Potato Knishes

Add 1 egg and baking powder to mashed potatoes. Then add flour, a little at a time, until the mixture is easy to handle and does not stick to fingers. To make the filling, sauté onion in oil until tender; add the chopped cooked meat and warm through. Remove from heat, add seasonings and 1 egg to bind. Take a small handful of the potato mixture, cup it in your hand, and add a heaping tablespoon of the filling. Fold the potato mixture around the filling, covering it completely. Bake on a greased baking sheet at 350° for 1 hour or until brown.

8 large potatoes, boiled and mashed
2 eggs
1 tsp. baking powder
¼–¾ cup flour
1 large onion, chopped
2 cups cooked chopped beef or poultry
Salt and pepper to taste

★

Ladino Fritada de Tomat

1 Tbsp. oil

2 (14 oz.) cans stewed
   tomatoes

½ tsp. sugar

2 slices soft bread crumbs

¼ lb. feta cheese, crum-
   bled

4 eggs, well beaten

1 cup grated Parmesan or
   Romano cheese

½ cup chopped parsley

eat oil in pan. Add tomatoes, mash them, and simmer until tomatoes are thick. Add remaining ingredients. Mix well. Pour into greased 6×9" or 8×8"
baking dish. Bake in 425° oven for 30 to 35 minutes until
brown on top.

☆

Entrées

Tu B'Shevat

Tu B'Shevat—the Jewish Arbor Day—is known as the New Year of the Trees and is a day of planting trees. The holiday has its origin in ancient spring agricultural celebrations, and one custom that has come down through the ages is the tasting of at least fifteen different types of fruits. The number is chosen because the holiday occurs on the fifteenth day of the month of Shevat, and occurs in January or February. A large variety of fruits, dried, fresh and in baked goods, are usually served.

Purim

The story of the Biblical Book of Esther is the merriest and most raucous of Jewish festivals. It is the only festival in which Jews are actually encouraged to drink alcoholic spirits. Purim celebrates a reversal of Jewish persecution.

Though the actual events in the Persian site are clouded in antiquity, and may never have actually happened, the message was considered so extremely important that it was included when the Bible was being codified. Purim is celebrated with costumed parties and merry rereading of the book of Book of Esther, complete with cheering and booing by the participants. Hamantaschen, triangular-shaped, filled hard pastries, are associated with Purim. The first written mention of the poppyseed honey mixture in connection with Purim is found in the medieval poem by Abraham Ibn Ezra, who lived in the early part of the 12th century. The choice of filling is yours, whether poppyseed, prune, or other.

Spicy Israeli Chicken

Mix cumin, paprika, salt and cayenne pepper. Rub the mixture thoroughly into the chicken pieces. Put them in a large bowl. Add onion, carrot, celery orange juice and wine. Cover and let stand 1 hour at room temperature or overnight in refrigerator.

Pat chicken pieces as dry as possible, reserving the marinade. Heat the oil in a large, heavy skillet. Add the chicken in batches and sauté over medium-high heat until brown on each side. Transfer the chicken to a shallow baking dish. Discard the fat from the skillet. Add the marinade with the vegetables to the skillet and bring to a boil, stirring.

Pour the mixture over the chicken, cover, and bake at 400° for 30 minutes. Uncover and bake 15 more minutes or until tender. Remove the chicken. Strain the cooking juices into a saucepan. Return the chicken to the baking dish, cover and keep warm.

Add the raisins and any juice that escaped from the orange segments to the cooking juices and boil until the raisins are tender and the sauce is concentrated and well-flavored. Whisk the water into the potato starch to form a smooth mixture. Add to the simmering sauce, stirring, and bring just back to a boil. Taste for seasoning. Add the orange segments, heat over low heat for a few seconds, and pour the sauce with the raisins and oranges over the chicken.

1½ tsps. ground cumin
1 tsp. paprika
½ tsp. salt
Pinch cayenne pepper
3½ lb. chicken, cut into serving pieces
1 onion, sliced thin
1 small carrot, sliced thin
1 celery stalk, sliced thin
1 cup orange juice
1 cup dry white wine
2 Tbsps. vegetable oil
½ cup dark raisins
2 Tbsps. water
2 tsps. potato starch or cornstarch
2 oranges, divided into neat segments, juice reserved

★

Yom Tov Chicken

2 broiler-fryer chickens,
  large, cut up
1 cup matzo meal
1 tsp. salt
  Dash pepper
½ cup peanut oil
2 cups onion, chopped
1 cup dried figs, sliced
  (about 8 oz)
4 cups applesauce
1 cup orange juice
2 tsps. grated orange rind
1 tsp. cinnamon
1 cup blanched almonds,
  slivered

R oll chicken parts in mixture of matzo meal, salt and pepper. Fry in hot oil in a large skillet until brown on both sides. Remove from pan. Drain off all but 2 tablespoons of the fat. Add onions; cook until tender. Return chicken to pan. Scatter fig slices around the chicken. Mix applesauce, orange juice, rind and cinnamon. Pour over chicken and figs. Cover and cook for 30 minutes or until tender. Add almonds. Cook for 5 minutes.

Serves 6–8.

Chicken Bernardino
(An early California Jewish recipe from the Gold Rush days)

auté chicken in oil. Mix remaining ingredients and pour on chicken. Bake in 325° oven for 45 minutes. Serves 4.

1 chicken, cut up
3 Tbsps. salad oil
1 (8 oz.) can tomato sauce
½ cup sherry
⅓ cup orange marmalade
¼ cup chopped onions
1 Tbsp. Worcestershire sauce

☆

Soy-Honey Chicken

½ cup soy sauce
½ cup honey
¼ cup dry sherry or apple juice
1 tsp. grated fresh ginger root
2 medium cloves garlic, crushed
1 broiler-fryer chicken (2½–3 lbs.), cut into serving pieces

ombine soy sauce, honey, sherry, ginger root and garlic in a small bowl. Place chicken into large glass baking dish. Pour honey marinade over chicken, turning to coat. Cover dish with plastic wrap. Marinate in refrigerator at least 6 hours, turning two or three times.

Remove chicken from marinade. Reserve marinade. Arrange chicken on rack over roasting pan. Cover chicken with foil. Bake at 350° for 30 minutes. Bring reserved marinade to a boil in small saucepan over medium heat. Boil 3 minutes and set aside.

Uncover chicken, brush with marinade. Bake, uncovered, 30–45 minutes longer or until juices run clear and chicken is no longer pink, brushing occasionally with marinade.

Substitute 2 tsp. ground ginger for the fresh ginger root, if desired.

Serves 4.

Chicken Casserole with Prunes

Put oil in deep 3 quart casserole. Add onions and sprinkle flour over onions. Put half the chicken pieces on onions. Sprinkle with salt and pepper. Add ½ of the prunes and 1 cup tomato sauce. Repeat layers of chicken, prunes and seasonings. Pour remaining sauce over the top. Cover and bake in a 350° oven for about 2 hours.

¼ cup vegetable oil
3 cups sliced onions
2 Tbsps. flour
2 frying chickens, cut up
Salt and pepper
1 lb. prunes
2 (8 oz) cans tomato sauce

Israeli Coffee Chicken

1 large broiler-fryer
  chicken, cut up
¾ cup coffee
⅓ cup ketchup
3 Tbsps. soy sause
2 Tbsps. lemon juice
2 Tbsps. wine vinegar
1 Tbsp. olive oil
2 Tbsps. brown sugar

Mix liquids and sugar, bring to a boil. Reduce heat and simmer 5–10 minutes to reduce. Pour over chicken in shallow baking dish and bake at 350°, uncovered, for 1 hour. Baste. Good served cold as well as hot.

Sweet Potato & Carrot Tzimmes

Brown the brisket. Place sweet potatoes in the bottom of a crock pot. Cover with grated carrots. Sprinkle brown sugar and cinnamon over the vegetables. Place brisket on top. Season with salt and pepper. Cover crock pot and cook on low setting for 8 to 10 hours.

2½ lb. fresh beef brisket
 2 lbs. sweet potatoes, peeled and quartered
 2 lbs. carrots, coarsely grated
 ⅓ cup brown sugar
 1 tsp. cinnamon
   Salt and pepper to taste
 1 cup water

What Is Tzimmes?

Tzimmes was a favorite New Year dish of Eastern Europe from the late medieval period. It is derived from the German Zummus, a compote or spicy vegetable concoction.

☆

Vegetarian Tzimmes

2 lbs. sweet potatoes, cut
up in chunks

2 lbs. carrots, cut up in
chunks

2 lbs. potatoes, cut up in
chunks

1 Tbsp. brown sugar

1 tsp. cinnamon
Salt and pepper to taste

2 cups water

1 Tbsp. Lyle's or Karo
dark syrup

3 sticks cinnamon

1 pinch ginger

1 lb. pitted prunes,
soaked overnight

 oil sweet potatoes, carrots, potatoes, brown sugar, cinnamon, salt and pepper for ½ hour or until very little liquid remains.

Add syrup, cinnamon sticks and ginger. Place the tzimmes in a covered Pyrex dish and bake at 350° for ½ hour. Uncover.

Add prunes and bake, uncovered, for another ½ hour.

☆

Lithuanian Prakkes (Stuffed Cabbage)

Place the raisins in a bowl and cover with wine. Soak them while you prepare everything else.

Fill a large pot with salted water and bring to a boil. Place the whole head of cabbage in the boiling water, cover the pot, reduce the heat, and simmer for 20 minutes. Remove cabbage from the water and drain in a colander. Pour cold water over the cabbage to stop it from cooking.

In a saucepan, bring another cup of salted water to a boil and add the rice. Parboil for 5 minutes. Drain in a colander and place in a mixing bowl. Cool to room temperature. When the rice has cooled, add the meat, eggs, salt and black pepper. Mix together well and set aside.

In a large, deep casserole, heat the oil over medium heat and sauté the onions until translucent and soft. Add the bay leaves, ginger, honey, apple, sugar, the raisins and their liquid, and the tomato sauce. Lower the heat to simmer and partially cover the pot. Simmer this mixture while you prepare the prakkes. The sauce should simmer at least 40 minutes, which will be just about the length of time it will take you to stuff the cabbage leaves.

Carefully peel off the leaves of the cabbage one by one, without tearing them. The leaves should be limp enough to enable you to do this easily, as well as to fold them over after you fill them. If necessary, cut off a small bit of the stem end of some of the leaves if you think they can be folded more easily with this removed. Do not discard these ends. They will be shredded together with the small leaves at the center of the head of cabbage and added to the sauce.

To stuff the cabbage leaves, place approximately ⅓ cup of the meat mixture into the center of a cabbage leaf. Spread it across so that when it is folded and rolled, it will form the shape of a cylinder or cigar. Fold the bottom (stem end) of the cabbage leaf over the stuffing. Then fold the two sides of either end across this fold. Roll the leaf, jelly roll fashion, across these folds and set it aside. Repeat this process with as many leaves as you can until all of the meat filling has been used up. You should be able to make between 16 and 20 cabbage rolls.

¾ cup raisins
1 cup red wine
1 large head green cabbage (or savoy cabbage)
⅓ cup rice
2 lbs. ground beef, lean
2 medium eggs
Salt and black pepper to taste
3 Tbsp. vegetable oil (corn oil or peanut oil is best)
2 large onions, peeled and very thinly sliced
2 bay leaves
1 1" piece fresh ginger, peeled and left whole
⅓ cup honey
1 tart green apple, peeled, cored, finely chopped or grated
⅓ cup brown sugar
6 cups fresh tomato sauce

continued on next page

☆

Lithuanian Prakkes (continued)

Preheat oven to 325°. After you have shaped and filled all the cabbage rolls, finely shred the remaining cabbage except for the core, which you may discard, and add it to the simmering sauce.

Gently lower the cabbage rolls, one by one, into the simmering sauce. Push them down as far as you can into the sauce, and make sure that after you have added all of the cabbage rolls they are as covered with sauce as possible. Cover the casserole tightly with aluminum foil and then with the lid of the casserole.

Transfer the casserole to the oven and bake for 2 hours. Recipe makes 6 to 8 servings.

What Are Prakkes, Holishkes, Golubtzes?

Prakkes *(also called* Holishkes *or* Golubtzes*)—stuffed cabbage—is one of the best known of the traditional Jewish dishes. It bears a great similarity to* Yaprakis, *the Greek-Jewish name for stuffed grape leaves. While Jews from all over the northern part of Eastern Europe make* prakkes *with a sweet-and-sour tomato sauce and raisins, those to the south, Hungary, Slovakia and Romania, prefer* golubtzes *with a savory tomato sauce that includes sauerkraut. Whatever you call them, whether you use them as a* forshpeis *(appetizer) or main meal, they are filling and delicious.*

Romanian Style Stuffed Cabbage

Directions for Mixture: Bring water to a boil in saucepan and parboil the rice 5 minutes. Drain it and put it in a mixing bowl. Heat oil in a small skillet over medium heat and sauté the onions until translucent and soft. Add garlic and paprika, reduce heat slightly, and cook for 5 minutes, stirring with a wooden spoon to prevent burning or sticking. Add this to the rice. Cool the entire mixture to room temperature. Add the meat, salt, pepper and egg and set aside while preparing the cabbage.

Directions for Cabbage and Sauce:

Fill a large pot with salted water and bring to a boil. Place the whole head of cabbage in the boiling water, cover the pot, reduce the heat, and simmer for 20 minutes. Remove cabbage from the water and drain in a colander. Pour cold water over the cabbage to stop it from cooking. Carefully peel off the leaves of the cabbage one by one without tearing them.

To prepare the sauce, first rinse and drain the sauerkraut in a colander to remove excess salt. In a large, deep casserole, heat the oil over medium heat and sauté the onions until translucent and soft. Add the two types of paprika and garlic, reduce the heat slightly, and cook 5 minutes longer. Add the bay leaf, sauerkraut, tomato sauce and wine, and partially cover the pot. Reduce the heat to simmer, and simmer gently while you stuff the cabbage leaves.

To stuff the cabbage leaves, place approximately ⅓ cup of the meat mixture into the center of a cabbage leaf. Spread it across so that when it is folded and rolled, it will form the shape of a cylinder or cigar. Fold the bottom (stem end) of the cabbage leaf over the stuffing. Then fold the two sides of either end across this fold. Roll the leaf, jelly roll fashion, across these folds and set it aside. Repeat this process with as many leaves as you can (usually 16 to 20) until all of the meat filling has been used up. Preheat the oven to 325°.

Shred all that remains of the head of cabbage except the core, and add it to the pot of simmering sauce. Then slowly lower the cabbage rolls, one by one, into the sauce. Push down as far as you can. Make sure that after all the cabbage rolls have been added, they are covered as well as possible by the sauce.

Cover the pot tightly with aluminum foil and then with its lid, and place it in the oven. Bake for two hours. To serve the cabbage rolls, serve 3 to each diner together with some of the sauce. Makes 6 to 8 servings.

Mixture:
- 1 cup cold water
- ½ cup rice
- 2 Tbsp. vegetable oil (corn oil is best)
- 1 medium sized onion, peeled and very finely chopped
- 2 cloves garlic, peeled and finely chopped
- 1½ tsps. paprika
- 1½ lbs. lean ground beef Salt and black pepper, to taste
- 1 large egg, beaten

Cabbage and Sauce:
- 1 large head of green cabbage (or savoy cabbage)
- 2 lbs. fresh sauerkraut
- 3 Tbsps. corn oil
- 1 large onion, peeled and very thinly sliced
- 1 Tbsp. Hungarian sweet paprika
- ¼ tsp. Hungarian hot paprika
- 2 cloves garlic, peeled and chopped
- 1 bay leaf
- 2 cups fresh tomato sauce
- ½ cup red wine

★

Polynesian Brisket

1 **fresh beef brisket**
1 **(12 oz.) can unsweet-
ened pineapple juice**
3 **Tbsps. soy sauce**
1 **pkg. dry onion soup mix**
3 **Tbsps. brown sugar**

Brown both sides of the brisket under the broiler. Mix the next four ingredients together. Pour mixture over meat. Cover tightly and roast at 350° approximately 2½ hours. Test with fork. Just before completely tender, slice. Return slices to marinade and return to oven to finish cooking (another ½ hour). Flavor is enhanced by leaving in marinade overnight in the refrigerator.

☆

Brisket with Prunes and Orange Juice

Place brisket in oven-proof casserole dish. Add all ingredients. Cover tightly with foil. Put lid on casserole and cook at 350° until tender. When cool, slice brisket. Place in serving dish in refrigerator. Refrigerate sauce as well. Remove fat from the top of the sauce, pour over sliced meat, reheat and serve.

1 beef brisket (approx. 3 lbs)
2 tsps. mixed herbs
2 cloves garlic, peeled
2 onions, chopped
2 bay leaves
1 lb. prunes
1 Tbsp. grated orange rind
2 tsps. salt
Freshly ground black pepper
2 cups boiling chicken stock
½ cup frozen orange juice concentrate

Boiled Beef

3 lbs lean beef (middle chuck, crosscut, short ribs, flank)
1 carrot, diced
2 stalks celery, diced
1 large onion, peeled
1 parsnip, diced
1 small white turnip, diced
3 bay leaves
6 peppercorns
1 Tbsp. salt
¼ tsp. paprika
2½ qts. boiling water
1 cup skinned fresh or canned tomato
¼ cup minced parsley

Braise the meat in the pot in which it is to be cooked until it is lightly browned on all sides. Add vegetables and cook for 5 minutes, stirring once or twice. Add remaining ingredients and cook over moderate heat, uncovered for 1½ to 2 hours or until meat is very tender. Remove meat and cut into serving portions. Serve hot with horseradish or tomato sauce. Strain the liquid and use for soup stock or serve with vegetables as a soup foundation. Serves 5 to 6.

Cholent

I n a large skillet brown the chopped onions. Add the meat and lightly brown. In a large pot (a turkey roaster) combine all the ingredients. Cover with boiling water and bake at 350° for the first hour. Reduce the temperature to 200° and leave for 8 to 10 hours. You can't overcook cholent. The longer you cook it the better. It is advised to check every 3–4 hours and add more boiling water when necessary and to correct seasonings.

2–4 Tbsps. vegetable oil
1 large onion, chopped
2 lbs. beef stew meat
5 lbs. potatoes, peeled
½ lb. dry lima beans
½ lb. barley
Salt and pepper
3 cloves garlic, chopped
Red pepper (optional)

What Is Cholent?

Cholent is a slow-cooking stew of beans, vegetables, potatoes and a small amount of meat served on the Sabbath afternoon. Cooking began, often in a communal oven, on Friday before the beginning of Sabbath since no work of any kind was allowed on the Sabbath.

Sweet and Sour Tongue

1 **fresh beef tongue**
4 **bay leaves**
6 **peppercorns**
1 **onion**
2–3 **carrots**
¼ **tsp. salt**

Sauce:
1 **large onion**
1 **Tbsp. chicken fat or
   vegetable oil**
1 **Tbsp. flour**
½ **tsp. salt**
1 **stick cinnamon or a
   dash of ground
   cinnamon**
¼ **cup chopped almonds**
¼ **cup seedless raisins**
¼ **cup brown sugar**
1 **Tbsp. maple syrup
   Juice of 1 large lemon**

oil tongue with bay leaves, peppercorns, onion, carrots and salt until soft. Skim, when necessary, as with soup. Skin, slice and arrange in a casserole dish. Reserve at least 3½ cups of stock.

Sauce: Sauté diced onion in oil until golden-brown. Sprinkle with flour. Add 3 cups of strained hot liquid, slowly, while stirring. Then add all the other ingredients and simmer for 10 minutes. Taste and add salt, if necessary. Pour over the tongue. (This can be left in the refrigerator for several days until needed).

When required, put in a 300° oven, uncovered for 1½ hours, basting occasionally. Add an occasional tablespoon of extra stock, if necessary.

Bavarian Pot Roast

Brown meat on all sides. Combine remaining ingredients. Pour over meat. Cover and simmer for three hours or until meat is tender. Thicken gravy with flour paste and serve over meat.

5 lb. chuck roast
1 Tbsp. cinnamon
1½ cups apple juice
1 (8 oz) can tomato sauce
1 Tbsp. vinegar
2 tsps. ginger
1½ tsps. salt
1 cup water
1 medium onion, minced (or 1 Tbsp. instant onion)
1 bay leaf
Flour paste for thickening

☆

Stuffed Breast of Veal

1 breast of veal with pocket cut

3 baking potatoes, cooked and coarsely mashed

1 lb. fresh spinach, chopped

2 large carrots, finely diced

1 onion, chopped

2 whole eggs, beaten (or equivalent egg substitute)

Salt, white pepper and paprika, to taste

¼ Tbsp. olive oil

2 garlic cloves, chopped

Braising ingredients:

1 quart veal or brown stock (canned beef broth)

2 onions, coarsely chopped

3 or 4 stalks of celery, chopped

1 large onion, chopped

Combine all stuffing ingredients to taste. Salt and pepper the inside of the cavity and fill, loosely. Stitch securely with butcher twine. Preheat olive oil in a large skillet until almost smoking. Brown roast on all sides, starting with fatty side. Remove from pan when brown and pour off oil. Pour braising liquid and vegetables over veal to cover ¾ of it. Cover pan securely. Place in a 375° oven for 1½–2 hours. Insert meat thermometer in the center of stuffing. When thermometer reads 165° to 170°, remove roast from juice. Remove vegetables from liquid and purée with liquid. Adjust seasonings. Slice, pour gravy over meat and serve.

Sweet and Sour Shoulder of Lamb

Remove as much fat from the lamb as possible. Mix stuffing ingredients. Make several incisions in the breast and fill with crumb mixture. Fry 2 quartered onions in oil. Add meat and brown on all sides. Season with salt and pepper. Add ½ cup stock. Cover tightly and place in 350° oven for 2½ hours. Meanwhile, make glaze by heating glaze mixture. Uncover meat and pour over half the glaze. Continue cooking. 15 minutes later, remove and place on serving platter. Make gravy by adding 1 cup of stock to pan drippings.

4–5 lb. shoulder of lamb
4 cloves garlic, slivered
½ cup raisins, preferably sultanas
1 tsp. thyme
1 tsp. marjoram
1 slice whole wheat bread, thick, crumbled
2 large onions, quartered
Cooking oil
Salt and pepper
1½ cup stock (beef or chicken broth)

Glaze:
2 Tbsps. apricot preserves or peach jelly or jam
1 Tbsp. lemon juice
2 Tbsps. brown sugar
2 Tbsps. Worcestershire sauce
2 Tbsps. tomato sauce

☆

Piquant Lamb

1 small shoulder of lamb
2 Tbsps. vegetable oil
1 large onion, sliced
1 tsp. salt
½ tsp. pepper
1 Tbsp. flour
1 cup dry white wine
1¼ cups stock (beef or chicken broth)
4 chopped anchovy fillets (optional)
1 Tbsp. parsley
1 clove garlic, chopped
Salt to taste
½ tsp. grated lemon rind

Remove as much fat from the lamb as possible. Place meat, oil and onion in heavy saucepan. Add salt and pepper. Brown meat slowly, but thoroughly, turning often to prevent burning. When brown, sprinkle with flour. add wine to the pan, and cook slowly until wine evaporates. Add stock. Cover saucepan and cook slowly for 1½ hours or until meat is tender. Add anchovies (optional), parsley, garlic, salt and lemon rind, stirring in gravy. Cook 1 minute, turning meat once.

Pink Spanish Rice

Bring last four ingredients to boil and add rice. Let it come to a boil again. Stir rice, cover, then bake at 350° for 15–20 minutes until done and water has evaporated. Remove from oven and fluff up with fork.

1 cup long grain rice
1 tsp. salt
1 tsp. vegetable or olive oil
2 cups water or chicken broth
2 Tbsps. tomato sauce

Sephardic Cooking

The history of the Sephardic Jews, the Jews from the Mediterranean, may not be as well known as that of the Ashkenazi Jews, those from Europe. The food is considerably different. Matzo balls, gefilte fish and bagels are not part of the Sephardic cuisine. Sephardic cuisine has more of a Mediterranean flavor.

At the time of the Spanish Inquisition in 1492, when Jews were required to convert to Christianity or were ordered to leave Spain, they fled to all parts of Europe. The Ottoman Turks welcomed them, knowing that they were educated and had contributed greatly to the Spanish Empire.

In fact, Sultan Mehmet II said, "They say the King of Spain is a wise man. I say he is a fool if he expelled the Jews. The Jews were the teachers, doctors, poets, bankers, and oiled the commerce of Spain." The Sultan then sent his own ships to pick up the Jews and transport them to Turkey.

After settlement in the Ottoman Empire, Sephardic Jews retained their old Spanish language, Ladino. Under Turkish, Greek and Italian rule, those Jews combined their Spanish food and the local food into what it is today.

☆

Yaprakis (Stuffed Grape Leaves)

1 small jar grape leaves,
   rinsed, drained, stems
   removed
1 cup white beans

Filling:
1 lb. lean ground beef
¼ cup rice
1 tsp. salt
   Pepper to taste
1 Tbsp. olive oil
¼ cup chopped parsley
2 Tbsps. tomato sauce

Sauce:
2 tsps. olive oil
¼ cup tomato sauce
2 cups water
   Juice of 1 lemon, added
   at end

Boil beans 30 minutes and drain. Mix filling ingredients together. On each grape leaf, vein side up, place a heaping teaspoon of filling and roll up in cigar shape, tucking in sides. In a casserole, place beans and rolls in layers, beginning and ending with beans. Make sure the rolls are placed close together. Pour sauce over all. Make sure sauce covers all. A few grape leaves may be added on top to cover. Cover pan and cook at 350° for 2–3 hours or until tender, adding lemon juice toward the end of the cooking. These taste even better when reheated the next day. Serve with Pink Spanish Rice recipe, above.

★

Köftes (Middle Eastern Meatballs)

Combine all ingredients. Make 15–18 patties in an oblong shape. Bake at 350° uncovered for 15 minutes, turn and bake an additional 15 minutes. Serve at room temperature with lots of lemon wedges as an appetizer, or serve hot with rice or bulgur pilaf. Serves 6.

1½ lbs. ground lamb
1½ tsps. dried mint leaves
1 cup bread crumbs, soft
1½ Tbsps. catsup
2 eggs
1 medium onion, finely chopped
½ tsp. salt
⅛ tsp. pepper
½ tsp. cinnamon
⅛ tsp. allspice

Esau's Stew

⅓ cup chopped onions
½ cup chopped celery
½ cup chopped carrots
5 Tbsps. butter or olive oil
5 cups water or stock
1 cup dried lentils
½ cup barley
⅛ tsp. rosemary
2 tsp. cumin
   Salt, to taste

In a large pot, sauté the onions, celery and carrots in the butter or oil. Add water or stock, lentils, barley and seasonings. Bring to a boil, turn down the heat and cook until barley and lentils are tender, about 1 hour. Serves 6 to 8.

★

Vegetarian Stew with Couscous

Heat 2 tablespoons oil in a Dutch oven over medium-high heat. Add eggplant and cook 4 minutes, stirring often, until lightly browned. Add zucchini and remaining oil. Cook 3 minutes, stirring once or twice. Add 1 can tomatoes, scallions, vinegar and seasonings. Cook 5 minutes or until vegetables are tender and most liquid has evaporated, stirring often. Add remaining can of tomatoes and chickpeas. Cook until hot. Remove from heat, stir in feta cheese, and serve over couscous. Serves 4.

- 3 Tbsps. olive oil
- 1 large eggplant, cut into ½" cubes
- 1 lb. zucchini, cut into ½" cubes
- 2 (14½"-oz.) cans Italian style cut up tomatoes, undrained
- 6 scallions, cut into ½" pieces
- 1 Tbsp. red wine vinegar
- 1 tsp. dried thyme
  Salt to taste
- ½ tsp. pepper
- 1 can chickpeas (garbanzo beans)
- 4 oz. feta cheese, diced
- 1 cup dry couscous, prepared according to package directions

☆

Passover Dishes

Passover

Passover, the eight-day spring festival, celebrates the deliverance of our ancestors from slavery in Egypt and our becoming a People. The first night of Passover is marked by a Seder, a home-centered ritual retelling of the Exodus story while enjoying a special meal complete with ritual foods. Children play an important part in this Seder, asking questions and learning the meaning and story of the symbolic foods. Passover is a combination of two ancient agricultural celebrations: a family celebration called the Pesach meal, dating back to desert days, from which our Seder developed, and the week-long Feast of the Unleavened Bread, which developed later as the Hebrews became farmers. It is a time to open our homes to our friends and members of the community.

We are told that during the Exodus, Jews fled in great haste and didn't have time to let their dough rise. This was because they baked it on their backs as they were running from Pharaoh. Matzo, the unleavened bread, reminds us of this flight and struggle. No leavened foods, legumes, or rice are served during the week. Products made from matzo replace any other grain. Not only are leavened foods not served, but they are removed from the house. In Sephardic homes, the same traditions are observed, but different foods are prepared, reflecting their Mediterranean background.

Traditionally, there is a Seder on each of the first two nights. On the second night, a Seder might be held at the Synagogue to allow the community to observe together and to insure that all who wish to attend a Seder have the opportunity to do. Feminist Seders are now becoming more common, giving women a chance to gather and retell their unique role in the deliverance.

Charoset (Sephardic Recipe)

6 dried Calimyrna figs

6 dates, pitted

2 Granny Smith apples

⅓ cup whole unblanched almonds, coarsely chopped

½ cup walnut halves, coarsely chopped

1 tsp. freshly grated ginger

½ tsp. cinnamon

1 Tbsp. honey

1 Tbsp. lemon juice

5 Tbsps. sweet kosher red wine

ut the tips of stems off figs and discard. Cut figs and dates into ¼" dice and place in medium bowl. Peel, core and cut apples into ¼" dice and add to dried fruit along with almonds, walnuts, ginger, cinnamon, honey and lemon juice.

Turn out the mixture onto a large wooden cutting board and chop until the mixture starts to come together. Drizzle wine over the mixture and continue to chop, forming a roughly textured, shiny paste.

Refrigerate in an airtight container until ready to serve. Can be made up to 6 hours ahead. Makes 3½ cups.

What Is Charoset?

Charoset is a combination of nuts, dried or fresh fruits, spices and sweet wine. Served on Passover with matzos and horseradish, it symbolizes the mortar used by the Hebrew slaves when they were working in Egypt.

Charoset (Ashkenazi Recipe)

Apples must be very finely chopped. Add nuts and cinnamon, with sufficient wine to make a mixture that holds together. Add cinnamon bark, if desired.

½ cup finely chopped apples
¼ cup chopped almonds or walnuts
1 tsp. cinnamon
Red Passover Wine (Manischewitz, Sosnick, etc.)
Cinnamon bark, if desired

☆

Chrain (Horseradish)

½ lb. horseradish root,
  peeled and grated
1 beet, peeled and grated
½ cup cider vinegar
¼ cup water
¼ cup sugar
½ tsp. salt

ombine ingredients and taste for seasoning. Place in jar. Keep tightly closed until time to serve.

Matzo Balls

Mix fat and eggs together. Mix and add matzo meal and salt. When well blended, add soup stock or water. Cover mixing bowl and place in refrigerator for at least 20 minutes.

Using a 3-quart pot, bring salted water to a brisk boil. Reduce flame until water bubbles slightly. Drop in balls formed from above mixture.

Cover pot and let cook 30 to 40 minutes. When soup stock or water is at room temperature or warmer, remove matzo balls from water to soup-pot. Allow the soup to simmer for 5 minutes before serving.

Recipe makes 8 balls.

- 2 Tbsp. chicken fat (or vegetable oil, but not olive oil)
- 2 eggs, slightly beaten
- ½ cup matzo meal
- 1 tsp. salt
- 2 Tbsps. soup stock or water

What Is Matzo?

Matzo, or unleavened bread, dates back to the Exodus from Egypt. In more recent history, Old World matzos were considerably different from those we buy in supermarkets today. Made and shaped entirely by hand in communal bakeries, those Matzos were either round or oval and much thicker than the commercial ones we now eat. The rich customers might tip the baker to secure thinner Matzos. Square matzos, later called "American-style matzos" were first made by machine in Austria in 1857. As late as 1912, they were still not manufactured in London and had to be imported from the Continent. The women of Italy took pride in shaping a perfect oval-shaped matzo, adding eyelets and festoons. Finely detailed, they could be made to look like pieces of art.

Matzo Brei

3 matzos
2 eggs
   Salt and pepper to taste
   Butter or margarine

reak the matzos into small pieces. Soak in warm water until soft and drain. Beat eggs and salt together and add the matzos.

Fry in butter or margarine until brown on both sides, or scramble. If you are making it pancake style, serve with jam and leave out the pepper.

Variation: Serve with sour cream, apple sauce or cinnamon sugar.

Stupendous Potato Kugel

Beat eggs. Mix potatoes, onions, baking powder, salt, pepper, matzo meal and ¼ cup of schmaltz, and quickly add to beaten eggs. Put remaining ¼ cup of schmaltz in a 9×13″ glass baking dish and heat in a 350° oven until sizzling. Then add kugel mixture and dot with a little bit of schmaltz. Bake at 350° for 1½ hours.

6 eggs
12 russet potatoes, grated
2 medium onions, finely chopped
1 tsp. baking powder
1 Tbsp. salt
¼ tsp. white pepper
1 cup matzo meal
½ cup plus 1 Tbsp. schmaltz, vegetable oil or Nyafat

☆

Matzo Kugel

6 matzos
2 Tbsps. melted
   margarine
6 eggs (or equivalent egg
   substitute)
1 (15-oz.) can
   unsweetened
   applesauce
½ cup granulated sugar
¼ cup milk (may be
   low-fat or nonfat milk)
   White raisins (or cut up
   dried fruit bits)
   Cinnamon and sugar
   to taste

Soak the matzos in warm water. Squeeze out the liquid. Toss with melted margarine. Beat eggs, add applesauce, sugar, milk and raisins. Mix together all ingredients. Spray a 2-quart pan with non-stick vegetable spray. Bake at 375° for 1 hour.

★

Mushroom Farfel Kugel

S auté the mushrooms, celery and onions in oil over medium heat until soft (10–15 minutes). Cover the matzo farfel with water and soak for a few minutes. Drain well in a colander. Mix the farfel, sautéed vegetables, salt and egg whites. Bake in a well-greased (non-stick vegetable spray) 8″ square baking dish, covered, in a 350° oven for 30 minutes.

½ lb. sliced mushrooms
1 celery stalk, chopped
1 medium onion, chopped
3 Tbsps. olive oil
4 cups matzo farfel (available in packages in markets)
1½ tsps. salt
2 egg whites

★

Sweet Matzo Farfel Kugel

1 cup boiling water
2 cups matzo farfel
2 eggs, beaten
¾ cup sugar
1 tsp. cinnamon
½ cup raisins
3 apples, pared and diced
½ cup walnuts, chopped
coarsely

our boiling water over farfel and soak for 5 minutes, covered, then drain. Mix farfel with all the remaining ingredients. Pour into a greased 9×13″ pan. Bake, uncovered, in a 350° oven for 45 minutes.

Farfel Stuffing

Mix farfel and warm water. Add salt. Sauté onion in a small amount of schmaltz. Add beaten egg. Mix in the mushrooms. Stuff chicken before roasting. Yields 2 cups of stuffing.

1 cup matzo farfel
¼ cup warm water
½ tsp. salt
1 small onion
   Chicken schmaltz or
   Nyafat
1 egg, beaten
½ cup chopped mush-
   rooms

✫

Passover Burmelos
(Sephardic Farfel Puffs)

2 cups farfel, soaked in
   water and squeezed dry
2 eggs, well beaten
½ tsp. salt
½ cup Parmesan cheese,
   grated
   Oil for deep frying

Mix all ingredients together. Drop mixture by table-spoonfuls into hot oil until golden brown on all sides. Drain on paper towels. They will be round and puffy. Serve hot with strawberry jam.

Spinaka

Crumble matzos into small pieces in a bowl and moisten with water until matzos begin to stick together. Mix in spinach, beaten eggs, feta cheese, oil, and all but ¾ cup of hard cheese.

Lightly oil 2 (10×18″) baking sheets completely. Divide mixture, covering pans evenly. Sprinkle reserved cheese over tops. Bake until crisp, 35 to 40 minutes at 350°.

1½ boxes matzos
4 packages frozen, chopped spinach, defrosted
4 large eggs, beaten
1 lb. feta cheese
½ lb. hard, sharp cheese (asiago or kassari), grated
½ cup canola oil

★

Passover Orange Chicken

1 egg
1 tsp. water
½ cup matzo meal
¾ tsp. salt
¼ tsp. pepper
1 frying chicken, cut up
1⅓ cups orange juice
12 prunes
1 orange, thinly sliced

Beat together 1 egg and 1 teaspoon water. Mix matzo meal, salt and pepper together. Dip chicken in egg mixture; roll in matzo meal to coat. Brown chicken pieces on all sides in a little oil. Add orange juice and prunes. Cover and simmer for 30 minutes, basting chicken occasionally. Add 1 thinly sliced orange and continue cooking 10 more minutes.

Brandied Chocolate Orange Torte

Preheat oven to 350°. Grease bottom of 8″ springform pan. Dust with cake meal, shaking off excess. Using electric mixer, beat yolks and ¼ cup sugar until slowly dissolving ribbon forms when beaters are lifted, about 5 minutes.

Combine raisins and ¼ cup cake meal. Fold raisin mixture, almonds, grated chocolate, juice, brandy and 1 Tbsp. peel into yolk mixture.

Using clean, dry beaters, beat whites with salt until soft peaks form. Gradually add remaining ¼ cup sugar and beat until stiff but not dry. Fold in yolk mixture. Turn into prepared pan.

Bake until tester inserted in center comes out clean, 55 to 60 minutes. Invert pan onto rack. Cool cake completely in pan. Remove springform. Garnish cake with peel and shaved semi sweet chocolate before serving.

Makes 8 to 10 servings.

Matzo cake meal (for pan)
4 eggs, separated
½ cup sugar
¾ cup raisins, chopped
¼ cup matzo cake meal
4 oz. toasted almonds, ground (¾ cup)
4 oz. semi-sweet chocolate, grated
6 Tbsps. fresh orange juice
2 Tbsps. Passover brandy
1 Tbsp. grated orange peel
Pinch of salt
Additional grated orange peel as garnish
Shaved semi-sweet chocolate as garnish

☆

Carrot Almond Cake

Matzo cake meal
(for pan)
4 eggs, separated
½ cup firmly packed light
   brown sugar
9 oz. carrots (1½ cups),
   finely grated
1 tsp. vanilla (optional)
¼ tsp. salt
½ cup sugar
1 cup finely ground
   toasted almonds
3 Tbsps. matzo cake meal
½ tsp. cinnamon

reheat oven to 350°. Grease bottom of 8" springform pan. Dust with cake meal, shaking off excess. Using electric mixer, beat yolks and brown sugar in large bowl until slowly dissolving ribbon forms when beaters are lifted, about 5 minutes. Stir in carrots and vanilla.

Using clean, dry beaters, beat whites with salt until soft peaks form. Gradually add sugar and beat until whites are stiff but not dry. Gently fold in yolk mixture.

Combine almonds, 3 Tbsps. cake meal and cinnamon. Fold gently into egg mixture. Turn into prepared pan, smoothing top. Bake until tester inserted in center comes out clean, about 1 hour. Immediately run knife around edge. Cool completely in pan on rack. Remove springform before serving.

Passover Walnut Torte

Beat egg yolks until lemon-colored. Add sugar and beat until fluffy. Add orange juice and rind. Sift flour and potato starch four times. Fold in gently to egg mixture.

Beat egg whites until stiff. Fold yellow batter into stiffly beaten whites. Add nuts. Bake 1 hour and 15 minutes at 325°.

 9 eggs, separated
1½ cups sugar
 ⅓ cup orange juice
    Rind of ½ orange
 ½ cup cake meal
 ⅓ cup potato starch
 ¾ cup ground walnuts

★

Passover Apple Torte

6 **large eggs, separated**
2 **cups plus 1 Tbsp. sugar**
¾ **cup matzo cake meal**
¾ **cup potato starch**
1 **cup apple juice**
1 **Tbsp. grated lemon rind**
½ **tsp. vanilla**
3 **large Granny Smith apples, cored and sliced**
1 **tsp. cinnamon**

n a large bowl, beat the yolks until they are thick and pale. Add 1¾ cups of the sugar gradually and beat the mixture until it is very thick.

Into a small bowl, sift together the matzo cake meal and the potato starch. Add the mixture to the yolk mixture alternately with the apple juice, beginning and ending with the matzo mixture and blending the mixture after each addition. Add the rind and the vanilla and beat the mixture until it is combined well.

Beat the whites until they hold soft peaks. Add ¼ cup of the remaining sugar, a little at a time, beating until they just hold stiff peaks. Stir ½ cup of the whites into the apple juice mixture and fold in the remaining whites, gently but thoroughly.

Pour the batter into a greased 9×13" baking pan, spreading it evenly, and arrange apple slices over it, overlapping slightly. In a small bowl, stir together the remaining 1 Tbsp. of sugar and the cinnamon and sprinkle the mixture over the apples. Bake in the middle of a preheated 325° oven for 50 to 55 minutes.

Passover Chocolate Nut Torte

Preheat oven to 350°. Beat egg yolks with sugar until thick (2 minutes on high-speed blender). Gently stir in walnuts, chocolate, apples and matzo meal. Beat egg whites until stiff. Fold into mixture. Bake in greased 9" springform pan for 1 hour. Cool in pan. Remove and dust top with powdered sugar before serving.

- 6 eggs, separated
- 1½ cups sugar
- 1 cup chopped walnuts
- 4 oz. semi-sweet chocolate, grated fine
- 2 Red Delicious apples, cored and grated
- ½ cup matzo cake meal
  Powdered sugar

★

Passover Farfel Cookies

2 cups sifted matzo cake meal
2 cups matzo farfel
1 cup chopped walnuts
1½ cups sugar
1 tsp. cinnamon
1 cup vegetable oil
4 beaten eggs

ix all ingredients together. Roll into balls. Flatten with fork and bake on a lightly greased cookie sheet for 25 to 30 minutes in a 350° oven. Makes about 4 dozen.

Passover Brownies

Melt chocolate and butter in the top of a double boiler. Beat the eggs with salt until thick. Add sugar, cake meal and nuts. Fold in chocolate mixture. Pour into a greased 8" square pan. Bake at 325° for 20 minutes. Cut while hot into squares.

3¾ oz. bittersweet
    chocolate
¼ cup butter
2 eggs
⅛ tsp. salt
⅔ cup sugar
½ cup matzo cake meal
½ cup walnuts, chopped

Baked Goods
& Desserts

Lag B'Omer

Lag B' Omer—the ancient grain harvest—was celebrated by bringing a measure, or Omer, of grain to the Temple. Various reasons are given for the seven-week period between Passover and Shavuot being a period of semi-mourning. Some say a plague occurred during this period, resulting in the sorrowful time. For whatever reason, Lag B' Omer, in the midst of the seven-week period, breaks the atmosphere. Festivities are encouraged and picnics, barbecues, dancing and the lighting of bonfires accompany the celebration. Traditionally, a boy's first haircut at the age of 3 will occur on Lag B.'Omer.

No special foods are associated with the holiday other than picnic foods, cakes, bagels, sandwiches and cookies. In Israel, chickpeas, falafel, fruits and nuts are popular fare.

Shavuot

Ushering in the summer, Shavuot is a spring harvest festival. In ancient days, it was one of the three great Pilgrimage festivals, when one was required to attend worship at the Temple in Jerusalem. It is traditionally the birthday of the Torah and celebrates the giving of the Law at Mt. Sinai. It concludes the spring cycle of holidays that began with the counting of Omer, a new sheaf of barley offered at the Temple, on the second day of Passover. Traditionally, the Book of Ruth is read on Shavuot. Set against the background of a harvest festival, it tells of a non-Jewish woman who became not only one of the Jewish people, but the one from whose family King David came. It symbolizes both the ingathering of the harvest and the gathering in of the people to the Law. First fruits and cheese blintzes and other dairy foods are eaten in honor of the Law, which is compared to "milk and honey."

What is Challah?

Challah is an Eastern European Yiddish name for a special loaf of bread baked fresh for the Sabbath. This tradition is so widespread among world Jewish communities that it may have had its roots in the Talmudic era. Over the centuries, the bread has assumed a variety of sizes, shapes and ingredients, depending on the customs of each region. Today, we are accustomed to a braided loaf that was adopted by the German Jews in the 16th and 17th centuries.

Challahs come in many shapes and sizes. For the average family, a one-pound braided challah may be just enough. But what could be more beautiful than a ten pound braided challah made for special celebrations? Challahs braided with three or five braids are those seen most often. For Rosh Hashanah, spiral challahs are made to symbolize the desire for a long life. In Eastern Europe, these round Rosh Hashanah challahs had a dough ring formed on the top to symbolize the hope for a complete and harmonious year.

For Shavuot, which commemorates the giving of the Torah, a challah might have a ladder on top to symbolize the ascent to Heaven. In the Ukraine, a bird's head would be shaped from dough and placed on top of the round Challah, symbolizing the phrase in Isaiah, "As birds hovering, so will the Lord of Hosts protect Jerusalem."

A round challah with a hand was created in Volhynia on Hoshana Rabba, symbolizing that, on this, the seventh day of Sukkot, the Judgment passed by God on Yom Kippur is confirmed by a written verdict and the hand of man is extended to receive it. A dough key was placed on an oval Challah in Volhynia for the first Sabbath after Passover. The key symbolized the gate of release which traditionally remains open for a month after the festival.

Jews from Lithuania baked challahs topped with a crown in accordance with the words "Let all Crown God." In Rhodes, challahs, called coulouri, are shaped in a ring.

Challah

Combine sugar, yeast and salt in large bowl. Whisk in water, eggs and butter. Add 3 cups flour and whisk until smooth, about 3 minutes. Using a wooden spoon, mix in enough remaining flour, ½ cup at a time, to form soft dough. Knead on floured surface until dough is satiny, about 10 minutes, kneading more if flour is sticky.

Grease large bowl. Add dough, turning to coat entire surface. Cover bowl with towel. Let it rise in a warm, draft-free area until doubled, about 1¼ hours.

Grease large baking sheet. Gently knead dough on lightly floured surface until deflated. For large loaf: Cut off ⅓ of the dough.* Cover both pieces with a towel and let them rest for 10 minutes to relax the gluten. Divide the larger piece of dough into 3 pieces. Roll each into a 14" rope. Braid together, working from the middle to the ends. Pinch the ends together. Place on prepared pan, tucking the ends under. Cut the remaining dough into 3 pieces. Roll each into a 9" rope. Braid together. Set smaller braid atop larger. Cover with waxed paper or towel. Let rise in a warm, draft-free area until doubled, about 45 minutes.

Preheat oven to 350°. Brush dough with egg glaze and sprinkle with poppy seeds or sesame seeds. Bake until golden brown and the bread sounds hollow when tapped on the bottom, about 50 minutes. Immediately transfer to rack and cool.

*For 2 medium loaves, cut the dough in half. Divide each half into 3 pieces. Roll each piece into an 8" rope. Form 2 braids. Transfer to 2 greased pans and let rise, as above. Bake about 45 minutes.

For variation, use 1½ to 3½ cups whole wheat flour to replace equal amount of all-purpose flour. Substitute honey for sugar. Dough may take a little longer to rise.

½ cup sugar
2 envelopes dry yeast
1 Tbsp. salt
1¼ cups warm water
4 eggs, room temperature
½ cup (1 stick) unsalted butter or margarine, melted and cooled
6 to 7 cups unbleached all-purpose flour or bread flour
1 egg, beaten with 2 Tbsps. milk or cream (glaze)
Poppy seeds or sesame seeds

Bagels

3 cups flour (plus
   3 Tbsps. for kneading
   board)
1½ tsps. salt
2 Tbsps. sugar
1 pkg. yeast
⅔ cup lukewarm water
3 Tbsps. salad oil
1 egg
4 quarts boiling water to
   which add 2 Tbsps.
   sugar

Optional topping:
   Poppy seeds, or
   Sesame seeds, or
   Coarse salt

 ift dry ingredients together into a deep mixing bowl. Dissolve yeast in ⅓ cup of the lukewarm water. Add oil to remainder of the warm water and stir into dissolved yeast. Make a well in the center of the flour mixture and stir in the liquid, adding slightly beaten egg when half the liquid has been used. Shape into a ball of dough and knead on a lightly floured board for two minutes.

Return dough to mixing bowl, smooth side up, and punch down three times. Cover and let rise at room temperature 15 to 20 minutes, or until the dough has come to top of bowl. Knead again in bowl until smooth and elastic. Divide dough into 12 equal portions. Form into lengths no more than ¾″ thick, pinching ends together. Place on a floured cookie sheet and place in broiler for 3 minutes. Remove from broiler.

Drop each bagel into rapidly boiling water in a deep kettle and cook over moderate heat 15 to 20 minutes. Skim out and place on cookie sheet. Bake at 375° for 10 minutes, then increase heat to 400° until bagels are browned and the crust is golden brown and crisp, 10 to 15 minutes. Makes 12 bagels.

Serving suggestion: Sprinkle poppy seeds, sesame seeds, or coarse salt over the bagels before baking.

Babka

Heat milk to lukewarm. Mix in yeast and 1 tsp. sugar. Set aside in draft-free place to proof (about 10 minutes). When proofed, mixture will be bubbly. Place 6 cups of flour, the remaining sugar, and the salt into a deep mixing bowl. Make a well in the center of the bowl and pour in the yeast mixture, orange juice and eggs. Beat together by hand or with hand blender. Add butter in small bits, beating and kneading all the while (about 30–35 minutes). The resulting dough will be much stickier than bread dough. If the dough does not look as though it will hold together, add up to ½ cup additional flour.

Grease a deep bowl with sweet butter and place the sticky dough into it. Cover the bowl with a damp kitchen towel and set aside to rise in a draft-free place for 1 hour or until the dough has doubled in bulk. Place the risen dough on a well-floured board or in a mixing bowl, and knead in the lemon and orange rind and the raisins.

Grease two large bundt or cake pans with butter. Sprinkle the pans with flour. Tip the pans from side to side in order to coat all sides of the pans with flour. Tap out excess flour. Pat the dough into the pans, making sure that all sides are even. The dough should be no higher than ¾ the height of the pans. Cover the pans with damp cloth and set aside for a second rising, about 1 hour. The dough will have risen to the top of the pans and will have doubled in volume.

Preheat oven to 350°. Bake the babkas in the oven for 40 to 45 minutes or until golden brown. Turn them out to cool on a wire rack before serving. To test for doneness, tap on the bottom. It should sound hollow. Serve babka with coffee or tea after it has cooled. Keeps well for several days.

9 to 9½ cups unbleached white bread flour
2 pkgs. freeze-dried yeast
½ cup sugar
6 eggs plus 2 egg yolks
2 sticks sweet butter, plus butter for greasing the rising and baking pans
½ tsp. salt
1½ cups golden raisins
Grated rind of 1 lemon and 1 orange
¾ cup orange juice, freshly squeezed
¾ cup whole milk

What Is Babka?

Babka is a semi-sweet yeast cake that was made all over Poland and Russia. It has always been a favorite of Jewish bakers from Eastern Europe, with its rich, velvety taste derived from the eggs and sweet butter used in the dough. The plain babka always had citrus peel and raisins in it. The fancier kinds had marbled layers of mocha, cocoa and cinnamon-sugar. The richest babka of all, shikkera babka (literally "drunk babka") was made with rum, whiskey or brandy and was served with hamantaschen on Purim.

☆

Hamantaschen

Pastry dough
- 1 **cup raisins**
- 2 **cups cold water**
- 1 **envelope freeze-dried yeast**
- ¾ **cup plus 1 Tbsp. sugar**
- 4½ **to 5 cups unbleached white bread flour**
- 1 **tsp. salt**
- 1 **cup vegetable oil or 1 stick sweet butter**
- 2 **eggs, beaten**

Poppy Seed Filling (**You may use Prune filling as an alternative**)
- 1 **cup poppy seeds**
- 3 **Tbsp. sugar**
- ⅓ **cup honey**
- ¼ **cup fresh-squeezed lemon juice**
- ½ **cup brandy or whiskey**
- ¼ **cup raisins**
  Finely grated rind of one lemon
- ¼ **cup blanched almonds, ground**
- 1 **egg white**
  Boiling water

irections for Pastry Dough: Place the water in a saucepan and bring it to a boil. Add the raisins and cook for 3 minutes. Cool to lukewarm. Drain the raisin water through a sieve into a container. This is called "raisin water." (You may dry and eat the raisins.)

Heat the raisin water to lukewarm. Dissolve the yeast with 1 Tbsp. of the sugar. Set aside in a draft-free place to proof. Yeast will be proofed in about 10 minutes, when the yeast will bubble up to the top of the glass in which it has been proofed.

Place 4½ cups of the flour into a mixing bowl. Use electric mixer or food processor to mix. Add all of the ingredients into the flour, mix, then knead either by hand or in the machine. Add more flour, if necessary, to achieve the correct texture, which should be smooth and moist, but not sticky. Finish kneading the dough by hand. Shape it into a ball and cover it with a damp cloth to begin the first rising.

Directions for Poppy Seed Filling:

Place poppy seeds in a heatproof mixing bowl. Pour enough boiling water over them to cover them by one-inch. Let them soak for 3 hours. Drain off excess water.

Place sugar, honey, lemon juice and whiskey or brandy in a saucepan. Stirring constantly, bring almost to a boil over medium heat. Stir until all the sugar and honey are dissolved, but do not let the mixture come to a boil.

Add drained seeds, raisins, lemon rind and almonds to the saucepan. Reduce heat to the lowest simmer, and simmer the ingredients 10 to 12 minutes, or until all the liquid has evaporated. Cool to room temperature. Beat the egg white until it forms stiff peaks. Fold this into the poppy seed mixture. The filling is now ready. (If you prefer, you may use the Prune filling instead of the poppy seed filling. Both are traditional).

Directions for Prune Filling: Soak the prune pieces and raisins in the wine for 1 hour. Place all ingredients in a food processor and, using a pulse/chop motion, grind into a paste. If the filling seems too liquid, increase the quantity of nuts until the consistency is correct. It should be a thick, compact paste.

★

Hamantaschen (continued)

D *irections for Hamantaschen*
Divide the yeast pastry dough into 3 parts. Roll out one part in a circle or rectangle ⅛" thick. Using a glass or a 2" cookie cutter, cut out 2" rounds. Fill each round with 1 tsp. of the poppy seed or prune filling. Place the filling in the center of the round of dough.

Pinch together 3 sides of each round of dough to form a triangular shape. Pinch the pieces together tightly so they won't break apart during baking. Using a pastry brush, brush the seal with a little cold water to fix it. Place each filled *hamantasch* on a well-greased cookie sheet. Repeat this procedure until you have used up all the dough and all the filling. As you fill a cookie sheet with *hamantaschen,* cover them with a damp kitchen cloth and set aside to rise until they are doubled in bulk, about 45 minutes.

Preheat the oven to 350°. Brush the *hamantaschen* with egg wash and bake 25 to 30 minutes. To test for doneness, lift up one hamantasch and tap it on the bottom. If it sounds hollow, it is ready. Cool hamantaschen on wire racks before serving.

Recipe makes about 36 *hamantaschen.*

Prune Filling (**Alternative to Poppy Seed filling**):
- 1 lb. pitted prunes, cut into bits
- ½ lb. dark raisins
- 1 cup walnuts
- ½ cup sweet red wine
  Juice and rind of 1 orange
  Juice of 1 lemon
- ⅓ cup honey

Hamantaschen
Pastry dough, as above
Poppy seed or Prune filling, as above
1 egg yolk mixed with 1 Tbsp. honey and 1½ Tbsp. water (egg wash)

★

What Are Hamantaschen?

Special pastry baked once a year in honor of the Purim holiday. Legend has it that the shape of hamantaschen resembles the three-cornered hat worn by Haman, minister to King Ahasuerus (Artaxerxes) of Persia.

The Book of Esther records that Haman had convinced the king to exterminate all the Jews of the Persian Empire because they would not declare him a god and bow down to him. Haman was exposed by the Jewish Queen Esther, with whom Ahasuerus was madly in love. Once he understood how he had been tricked, King Ahasuerus ordered that instead of the Jews, Haman should be hung on the gallows. After this happened, Jews all over the world began to celebrate Purim in remembrance of the triumph of good over evil.

In all truth, it is highly unlikely that Haman wore a three-cornered hat. This was a fashion in eighteenth century Europe, where the Jewish folktale originated, and not in ancient Persia. Also, hamantaschen is a Yiddish, not a Hebrew word.

The true origin of the word hamantaschen comes from the medieval German term mohn taschen (poppy seed pockets). These pockets may or may not have been triangular in shape when the recipe was first conceived, but this dish was adopted and brought east by Jews from Germany into what would become Yiddish-speaking Eastern Europe. Because the expression mohn taschen reminded Jews of Haman's name, the name hamantaschen (Haman's pockets) was given by Jews to this pastry and it came to be baked in honor of Purim.

Mandelbrot (Mandel Bread)

Cream eggs and 1 cup sugar in mixer. Add oil, juice, or juice and liquor, and beat in lightly but completely. Add orange rind, 4½ cups flour, baking powder and ground almonds. Beat in. Knead in the sliced almonds. The dough should be dry enough to work with easily: soft and pliant, not sticky. If it is too loose or too sticky, add up to ½ cup additional flour.

Preheat oven to 350°. Place oven rack on middle shelf. You will need several well-greased cookie sheets.

Divide dough into 3 parts. Shape each part into a 2"–diameter log. Place each of these on a well-greased baking sheet. Bake 1 or 2 of the logs at one time for 30 to 35 minutes or until nicely browned. Remove logs from oven and cool slightly. Slice each log into ½"–thick slices. Lay each slice on a well-greased cookie sheet. Each slice should reveal almonds attractively floating in the dough.

Beat egg white and water. Mix remaining sugar with cinnamon. Set each of these next to you with a pastry brush while you work on the next steps.

Lay slices of mandelbrot across the cookie sheet, cut-side up. Bake for 5 minutes. Remove mandelbrot from oven and turn each slice over. Brush top with beaten egg white and sprinkle with cinnamon-sugar mix. Return mandelbrot slices to oven and bake for another 5 minutes. Repeat this until all of the mandelbrot has been baked twice, once with the cinnamon-sugar coating. Cool to room temperature and store. Makes about 4 dozen mandelbrot slices.

4 eggs plus 1 large egg white, beaten with
1 Tbsp. cold water
1¼ cups sugar
1 cup corn oil or peanut oil
½ cup freshly squeezed orange juice or
¼ cup orange juice plus
¼ cup whiskey, brandy or amaretto liqueur
Rind of 1 orange, finely grated
4½–5 cups unbleached cake flour
1 tsp. baking powder
¾ cup finely ground almonds
1½ cups sliced unblanched almonds
½ tsp. ground cinnamon

Marta's Cookies (German Blaetter Teig)

8 oz. cream cheese
2 cubes sweet margarine
3 egg yolks
2 cups flour
  Raspberry jam or
  marmalade
  Flour, egg yolk, sugar,
  for baking

Cream cream cheese and margarine. Add egg yolks and gradually add flour. Refrigerate dough overnight. Cut dough in half and return unused half to the refrigerator. Roll dough ¼" thick and cut into rounds approximately 2½" in diameter. Make cookie sandwiches by using 2 rounds of dough and filling them with either raspberry jam or marmalade. Sprinkle cookie sheet with flour. Brush cookies with egg yolk and sprinkle with sugar. Bake until light brown, about 20 to 25 minutes at 350°.

Strudel

Cream butter and margarine with egg yolk. Mix in sour cream and flour. Make a ball. Wrap in waxed paper and put in the coldest part of refrigerator overnight. Roll out on floured board very thin. Sprinkle with nuts, raisins and cinnamon. Make a thin layer of preserves over the nuts, raisins and cinnamon. Sprinkle lightly with bread crumbs. Roll up in a long strip. Spread top with egg white. Bake on ungreased cookie sheet at 350° until light brown.

The same dough may be used to make Rugelach. Cut into squares and sprinkle with sugar, cinnamon, nuts and raisins. Roll up from a corner to form a crescent shape. Dip into egg white and then into sugar and cinnamon. Bake at 350° until light brown.

¼ lb. butter
¼ lb. margarine
1 egg yolk
1 cup sour cream
2 cups flour
  Nuts
  Raisins
  Cinnamon
  Apricot preserves
  or cherry-pineapple
  preserves
  Bread crumbs
1 egg white
  Powdered sugar

Mom's Plum Kuchen

4 Tbsps. butter, plus more for pan
1 cup flour, plus more for pan
½ tsp. baking powder
1 egg, plus 1 yolk
2 Tbsps. milk, plus
3 Tbsps. milk
Prune plums
¼ cup sugar
Cinnamon
Nutmeg

Cut butter into dry ingredients. Add egg and then milk. Butter and flour a springform pan. (You may also use a 9"–square pan). Pat dough to line bottom of pan. Keep flouring fingers.

Quarter plums. (You may also use apples, nectarines or apricots). Sprinkle sugar, cinnamon and nutmeg on them. Line the dough with fruit, setting it in neat rows or in circular patterns. Mix 1 egg yolk and 3 Tbsps. milk, beating lightly. Pour over the fruit. Bake for 20 to 30 minutes in 400° oven.

My Mother's Jewish Apple Cake

Sprinkle 5 Tbsps. sugar and 2 tsps. cinnamon on apples and set aside. Sift together 3 cups flour, 3 tsps. baking powder, and salt. Cream oil and 2 cups sugar. Add orange juice, vanilla, eggs and flour mixture to sugar mixture. Grease tube pan. Pour ½ of the batter in the pan, top with ½ of the apples. Add the rest of the batter, then the rest of the apples. Bake at 325° for 2 hours or until brown. Cover lightly with foil after 1 hour to prevent over-browning. Cool overnight in upright position.

Freezes well.

5 Tbsps. sugar
2 tsps. cinnamon
5–6 apples, peeled and sliced
3 cups flour
3 tsps. baking powder
1 tsp. salt (optional)
1 cup vegetable oil
2 cups sugar
¼ cup orange juice
1 Tbsp. vanilla
4 eggs

Linzer Torte

1½ cups almonds,
    unblanched
½ cup butter or margarine
    plus 2 tsps.
⅔ cup sugar
 1 egg
½ tsp. vanilla
½ tsp. lemon peel, grated
 2 cups flour, unsifted
½ tsp. baking powder

Fruit filling:
 6 cups fruit (fresh berries
    or peaches, plums,
    apricots or nectarines)
¾ to 1¼ cups sugar
    (depending on sweet-
    ness of fruit)
 1 Tbsp. lemon juice
 1 stick cinnamon
    (optional)

I n a blender or food processor, whirl nuts until finely ground. Put aside. Beat butter and sugar until light and fluffy. Add egg, vanilla and lemon peel. Beat to blend. Stir together flour, baking powder and ground nuts. Gradually add to creamed mixture, beating well. (If you have a heavy-duty mixer, beat in all flour—nut mixture; otherwise stir in mixture with a spoon). Cover and chill at least 30 minutes, but it can wait overnight.

To form crust, divide dough into thirds. Return ⅓ to refrigerator and press remaining dough evenly over the bottom and sides of a 12" tort-pan with removable bottom, or a 12" pizza pan.

Fruit filling: Place 6 cups of fruit in saucepan. Depending on the sweetness of the fruit, add ¾ to 1¼ cups of sugar, 1 Tbsp. of lemon juice and 1 stick of cinnamon (optional). Boil quickly, stirring frequently to prevent sticking, over low to medium-low heat, until jam is thick and reduced to about 2 cups. This takes 45 minutes to 1 hour. (As a short cut, begin with jam; heat and add 1 Tbsp. lemon juice and cinnamon stick).

Spread filling over dough. With reserved third of dough, gently roll strips about ¼" thick on a lightly floured board. Form lattice over top. If strip breaks, just pinch it back together. Bake at 350° for 30 minutes or until crust is lightly browned.

Roslyn's Chocolate Puff Meringues

Line baking sheet with foil. Beat egg whites and salt until stiff. Gradually beat in sugar. Stir in chips, cocoa and vanilla. Drop batter by walnut-sized spoonfuls onto prepared baking sheets. Bake for 30 minutes at 275°. Transfer entire foil to rack to cool. Store in air-tight container.

3 egg whites
Pinch salt
1 cup sugar
1 (6 oz.) pkg. mini-chocolate chips
2 Tbsps. unsweetened cocoa powder
½ tsp. vanilla

My Italian Grandmother's Jewish Coffee Cake

8 oz. sour cream
1 tsp. baking soda
1 stick butter
1 cup sugar
2 eggs
¼ tsp. salt
1 tsp. vanilla
1½ cups flour, sifted
1 tsp. baking powder

Topping:
½ stick butter
½ cup flour
4 Tbsps. brown sugar
4 Tbsps. sugar
½ tsp. cinnamon
¼ tsp. salt
½ tsp. baking powder
½ cup walnuts, chopped

Mix sour cream and baking soda and let stand. Cream butter and sugar. Add eggs, one at a time, beating well after each one. Add salt, vanilla, and sour cream mixture. Mix well. Add flour and baking powder. Beat well. Mix all topping ingredients with pastry blender until butter is crumbly. Pour ½ cake mix into 9×13" pan and cover with ½ of the topping. Add the rest of the cake mix and finish with the rest of the topping. Bake at 350° for 40 to 45 minutes.

Chocolate Chip Coffee Cake

Cream together butter, sugar, eggs and sour cream. Sift dry ingredients together and add to the first mixture along with the vanilla.

Combine brown sugar, chocolate chips and nuts together to make the filling. Grease and flour an angel food cake pan. Pour In a little less than half of the batter. Sprinkle with a little less than half of the filling. Add the remaining batter and top with the remaining filling. Bake at 350° for 45 to 50 minutes.

¼ lb. butter
1 cup sugar
2 eggs
8 oz. sour cream
2 cups flour
1 tsp. baking soda
1 tsp. baking powder
1 tsp. vanilla
½ cup brown sugar
1 small package chocolate chips
½ cup nuts

Spicy Marble Coffee Cake

½ cup margarine
¾ cup sugar
1 egg
2 cups flour
2 tsps. baking powder
½ tsp. salt
¾ cup milk
2 Tbsps. molasses
1 tsp. cinnamon
¼ tsp. nutmeg
½ tsp. ground cloves

Nut topping mix:
½ cup brown sugar
½ cup walnuts
2 Tbsps. flour
1 tsp. cinnamon
2 Tbsps. butter, melted

C ream margarine and sugar. Add egg and beat well. Sift flour, baking powder and salt. Add to creamed mixture, alternating with milk. Divide into 2 parts. To 1 part, add molasses and spices. Spoon batters alternately into greased 8" pan. Zigzag spatula through. Sprinkle with nut topping mix. Bake in moderate oven at 350° for 40 to 45 minutes, until done.

Orange Sponge Cake

Separate eggs. Beat whites well, but not dry. Add ¾ cup sugar. Beat until stiff. Beat egg yolks until lemon-colored. Add 1 cup sugar and mix well. Add orange juice. Add sifted dry ingredients. Fold yolk mixture into beaten whites. Pour into tube pan. Bake at 325° for 1 hour and 10 minutes. Invert.

- 7 large eggs
- 1¾ cups sugar
- ½ cup warm orange juice
- 2 cups flour
- 1 rounded tsp. baking powder
- 1 tsp. cream of tartar

Banana Cake

¾ cup butter
2 cups sugar
3 eggs
6 rounded Tbsps. sour cream
3 large bananas, mashed
2¼ cups regular flour, sifted
1½ tsps. baking soda
½ tsp. salt
1½ tsps. vanilla

ream butter and sugar. Add eggs and beat in. Add sour cream and beat in. Add mashed bananas. Sift flour, baking soda and salt together. Add this to the mixture and beat well. Add vanilla.

Grease and flour a bundt pan. Pour in the cake mixture. Bake for 1 hour and 10 minutes in a 350° oven. After removing from the oven, allow the cake to stand in the pan for 30 minutes before inverting onto a wire rack.

Aunt Faye's Honey Cake

Combine all ingredients into one large bowl and mix well. Add nuts and raisins at end if desired. Line an 11×13" pan with waxed paper. Bake at 325° for 50 minutes.

1 cup sugar
⅔ cup vegetable oil
3 eggs
1 lb. honey
1 cup black coffee, cold
3½ cups flour
1 tsp. baking powder
1 tsp. baking soda
½ tsp. nutmeg
½ tsp. cinnamon
    Nuts and/or raisins
    (optional)

☆

Perfect Pear Kuchen

Almond Topping
- ¾ cup firmly packed dark brown sugar
- 1 Tbsp. bleached all-purpose flour
- ½ tsp. freshly ground cardamom
- 2 Tbsps. (¼ stick) well chilled unsalted butter
- 1 cup chopped, toasted unblanched almonds

Cardamom Cake
- 2 cups sifted bleached all-purpose flour
- 1 tsp. baking powder
- 1 tsp. baking soda
- 1 tsp. freshly ground cardamom
- ¼ scant tsp. salt
- ½ cup (1 stick) unsalted butter, room temperature
- 1 cup sugar
- 3 eggs, room temperature
- 1 tsp. grated lemon peel
- 1 cup sour cream, room temperature
- ¾ lb. pears, peeled, cored and cut into ⅓ to ½" dice

or topping: Blend sugar, flour and cardamom in medium bowl. Cut in butter until coarse meal forms. Mix in chopped almonds. Set aside.

For cake: Position rack in center of oven and preheat to 325°. Grease 9×13" ovenproof glass baking dish. Sift first 5 ingredients into bowl. Using electric mixer, cream butter in another bowl. Add sugar and beat until light and fluffy. Beat in eggs, 1 at a time. Mix in lemon peel. Blend in dry ingredients alternately with sour cream, beginning and ending with dry ingredients. Smooth batter in prepared dish. Top with pears. Sprinkle with topping. Bake until tester inserted in center comes out clean, about 40 minutes. Cool 25 minutes. Serve warm or at room temperature. Makes 10 servings.

★

Best Ever Brownies

Combine chocolate, margarine, butter and espresso powder in top of a double boiler over simmering water. Melt, stirring occasionally. Remove from heat. Add sugar, eggs and vanilla. Mix well. Sift together flour and salt and add to chocolate mixture. Stir well and fold in nuts. Pour into greased and floured 9" square pan. Bake in 350° oven for 45 minutes. When done, brownies will be glossy, but inside should be moist.

Mint Frosting: Cream butter and mix powdered sugar. Add enough cream to make smooth and add flavoring and food coloring. Spread on cooled brownies and freeze 15 minutes.

Topping: Drizzle on top 2 squares baker's chocolate, melted and mixed with 2 Tbsps. butter.

4 squares unsweetened chocolate
¼ lb. unsalted butter
¼ lb. unsalted margarine
1 Tbsp. instant espresso
2 cups sugar
3 eggs, well beaten
1 tsp. vanilla
1 cup flour
¼ tsp. salt
1 cup chopped pecans

Mint Frosting
3 Tbsps. butter or margarine
1½ cups powdered sugar
1½ Tbsps. cream
1¼ tsps. peppermint extract
Red food coloring

Topping:
2 squares baker's chocolate, melted
2 Tbsps. butter

☆

Poppy Seed Cake

¾ **cup poppy seeds**
¾ **cup milk**
¾ **cup butter**
1½ **cups sugar**
4 **egg yolks**
3 **cups flour**
2 **tsps. baking powder**
1 **tsp. vanilla**
4 **egg whites, beaten stiff**

Soak poppy seeds overnight in the ¾ cup milk. Cream butter and sugar and add egg yolks. Beat until smooth. Alternate the sifted dry ingredients with the poppy seeds that have been soaked in milk. (Note: If the batter is a little thick, add another ¼ cup of milk). Add vanilla. Add the stiffly beaten egg whites slowly. Bake in a 9" greased tube pan for 45 minutes at 350°. Let cake cool before removing from pan. Frost with your favorite frosting.

Marta's Cheesecake

Cut margarine into the flour. Stir in the egg yolks and the rest of the cheesecake ingredients and knead the dough. Let the dough rest in the refrigerator at least overnight. Can be kept in the refrigerator for about 1 week. Divide dough in two and pat the dough evenly into buttered springform pans. It should be ¼" thick. Make a roll of the dough, about ¼" thick, and press evenly and tightly around the edge of the pans.

Cheese filling: Separate the egg yolks, keeping the whites in the refrigerator. Put yolks in a blender and add the sugar. Slowly add the cottage cheese, then rum and brandy. Mix until fluffy and almost liquid. Cut the cream cheese into about 5 pieces and add them one at a time. Then add the baking powder. Beat the egg whites in a large bowl until stiff. Fold this into the cream cheese mixture and pour into the prepared dough. Bake for 1½ hours at 325°. Yields 2 cakes of about 9½ inches.

8 oz. unsalted margarine
 or butter
2 cups flour
3 egg yolks
1 cup sugar
2 Tbsp. lemon juice
1 Tbsp. rum
1 Tbsp. brandy

Cheese filling:
4 eggs
1 cup sugar
16 oz. low fat cottage
 cheese
1 Tbsp. rum
1 Tbsp. brandy
8 oz. cream cheese
1 tsp. baking powder

☆

Creamy Cheesecake

12 oz. cream cheese
2 eggs, beaten
¾ cup sugar
2 tsps. vanilla
½ tsp. lemon juice
   Graham crust

Topping:
1 cup sour cream
3½ Tbsps. sugar
1 tsp. vanilla

Combine cheesecake ingredients. Beat until light and frothy. Pour into graham crust and bake at 350° for 15 to 20 minutes. Remove and cool for 5 minutes, then pour topping over cheesecake and bake for 10 minutes more.

Chocolate Cheesecake

Combine wafer crumbs and butter. Press mixture into the bottom of a 9″ springform pan and set aside. In a small saucepan, heat the water to a boil. Reducing heat to low, add chocolate pieces and stir until melted. In a large bowl, cream cheese until light and fluffy. Add sugar and eggs and continue beating until well blended. Add melted chocolate and beat at low speed. Add sour cream and vanilla and continue beating until well blended. Pour batter into prepared pan. Bake at 350° for 55 to 60 minutes. The sides will be puffed and the center soft. The cake will firm as it cools. Place cake on a wire rack and cool for several hours before removing the sides of the pan. Garnish with powdered sugar and chocolate curls. Serve at room temperature.

To freeze: Wrap well and freeze for up to four months. Thaw at room temperature for 3 to 4 hours before serving.

1 cup crushed chocolate wafers (about 20)
¼ cup margarine or butter, melted
¼ cup water
1⅓ cups semi-sweet chocolate chips
3 (8 oz.) packages cream cheese, at room temperature
1 cup sugar
2 eggs
1 cup sour cream
1 tsp. vanilla
Powdered sugar and chocolate curls, as garnish

An Old Family Recipe for Apple Pie and Pie Crust

Pie crust: (Makes 2)
- 2 **cups flour**
- 1 **cup vegetable shortening**
- ½ **cup water, milk or juice**

Apple pie filling:
- 5 **to 7 cups apples, cored, peeled and thinly sliced**
- ¾ **cup sugar (or less)**
- 1 **tsp. lemon juice**
- ½ **tsp. cinnamon**
- ¼ **tsp. nutmeg**
- 1 **pinch salt**
- 1 **Tbsp. flour**
- 1 **Tbsp. butter**

Put flour in mixing bowl, cut in shortening quickly to size of small peas. Moisten mixture with liquid until it just holds together. Form into ball with hands. Be sure to flour rolling pin and dough lightly to prevent sticking. Crust may also be rolled out between two sheets of waxed paper, lightly floured.

Cut dough into two parts, one slightly larger than the other. Place on a lightly floured board and pat quickly into a thick, flat disk. Roll lightly from the center out, in all directions (about ⅛" thick). Lift pastry into pan without stretching. For a well-baked bottom crust, pre-bake shell in hot oven for 5 minutes.

Mix thinly sliced apples with all ingredients except butter. Put in a pastry-lined pan, heaping high in the center. Dot with butter. Moisten edge of bottom crust, cover with top crust, flute or press with tines of a fork. Make several slits in top crust. Bake in 450° oven for 15 minutes. Reduce heat to 350° and bake 35 minutes or until crust is brown or until juice bubbles through slits on top of pie.

☆

Double Ginger Gingerbread

Position rack in center of oven and preheat to 350°. Grease 8″ square baking pan; dust with flour. Sift first 8 ingredients into bowl. Using electric mixer, cream butter in another bowl. Add brown sugar and beat until light and fluffy. Beat in egg, then molasses. Mix in buttermilk alternately with dry ingredients. Fold in crystallized ginger and orange peel. Spoon batter into prepared pan. Bake until springy to touch, 45 to 50 minutes. Cook cake in pan on rack. Serve with cream.

Directions for Grand Marnier Cream: Beat cream, Grand Marnier and vanilla until beginning to thicken. Add sugar and sour cream and beat until soft peaks form. Serve immediately.

2 cups sifted unbleached all-purpose flour
1½ tsps. cinnamon
1 tsp. ground ginger
1 tsp. baking powder
½ tsp. baking soda
¼ tsp. salt
⅛ tsp. cardamom
⅛ tsp. ground cloves
½ cup (1 stick) unsalted butter, room temperature
½ cup firmly packed dark brown sugar
1 egg
¾ cup light molasses
¾ cup buttermilk
3 Tbsps. minced crystallized ginger
1 Tbsp. grated orange peel

Grand Marnier Cream
⅔ cup well-chilled whipping cream
2 tsps. Grand Marnier
1 tsp. vanilla
3 Tbsps. sugar
3 Tbsps. sour cream

★

Roslyn's Chocolate Mousse

6 oz. semi-sweet
   chocolate
   A few Tbsps. of water
1 Tbsp. brandy or rum
4 eggs, separated
1 tsp. vanilla
   Wafer cookies and
   whipped cream to
   decorate

I n top of double boiler, heat chocolate with a few Tbsps. water and brandy or rum (alcohol will cook off). Stir until melted and set aside.

Separate eggs. Beat whites until stiff and set aside. Beat yolks until thick and lemon-colored.

Beat chocolate into yolks with vanilla. Fold in the whites. Begin with a small amount of whites, mixing slightly, then gradually add the rest of the whites, folding gently to keep the air in—hence the "mousse" effect.

Spoon into 4 individual dishes and chill overnight. Serve with a small wafer and whipped cream if desired.

Israeli Spiced Fruit

P lace figs in a large saucepan and cover with warm water. Soak for 1 hour, then drain. Add enough water to cover the figs by 3". Place over medium heat and simmer until just soft, 5 to 10 minutes. Add prunes, apricots, raisins, sliced lemon, cinnamon sticks and sugar. Simmer over low heat, stirring gently, until sugar dissolves, about 5 minutes. Remove from heat. Add pine nuts, lemon juice and enough water to cover the fruit by 3". Refrigerate, covered, for several days to allow the fruits to absorb the liquid and develop flavor. Serve chilled, at room temperature, or warmed. Pass the cream for drizzling over the top if desired.

1½ cups dried figs, preferably white, stems removed
1½ cups pitted prunes
1½ cups dried apricots, nectarines or pears
¾ cup golden raisins
1 lemon, thinly sliced, cut into half circles
2 3" cinnamon sticks
½ cup sugar
½ cup pine nuts
⅓ cup lemon juice
Heavy (whipping) cream —optional

☆

Two Twentieth-Century Jewish Holidays

Yom Ha'Shoah

Yom Ha'Shoah is the most recent solemn day in the Jewish calendar. This day, which falls in early May of each year, is as somber as Tish B'av, which commemorates the destruction of the First and Second Temples. Yom Ha'Shoah commemorates the death of the six million Jews in Europe under Adolf Hitler's Nazi Regime between 1933 and 1945.

Fully one out of every three Jews in the world perished during the terrible time of the Holocaust. Jews observe this day with readings and remembrances and lighting of candles for those slain, so that we might never forget what happened during those terrible times and guard that they might never again occur.

Yom Ha'Atzma'Ut

After the mass destruction of European Jewry in the Holocaust, the Jewish people felt they might never recover. Yet in May, 1948—three years after the end of World War II—the 2000-year-old dream of people who had been dispossessed of their land and dispersed to other lands (Diasporah) came true when, in May 1948, the Jewish State of Israel—the first and only nation peopled by a majority of Jews—was reborn. Yom Ha'Atzma'Ut celebrates the birth of Israel. It is akin to the American Fourth of July.

Secrets of the Professionals

Restaurants and Delicatessens from the Four Corners of North America

What Makes This Cookbook Different? The Professionals!

ome Jewish cookbooks contain the recipes of one or a few Jewish families handed down from generation to generation. Others gather their recipes from Synagogues, Sisterhoods, Hadassah, and the like.

In this cookbook, we have gone one step further: We have selected delicatessens and restaurants—professional purveyors of Jewish food—throughout the nation, and they have generously given of their expertise. Since these establishments have shared only a few of their many secrets with us, we strongly recommend that you visit them to see what other delicacies they serve to tempt your palate.

Some of the professional recipes are for the same foods you'll find in earlier sections of this book—latkes, matzo balls and noodle kugel are prime examples. Indeed, some of the deli/restaurants themselves have overlapped in their recipes. But, in the true Jewish tradition, this is just fine, since each Jewish cook considers himself or herself to possess "the only" and "the best" recipe in existence! Thus, we suggest that you might enjoy trying different recipes for the same dish and see which one you like best. That way you can insure, once and for all, that you—and no one else—knows the best and only recipe for this dish in the whole wide world.

In Judaism, a Minyan—traditionally ten adult males, but more recently ten adults—is the minimum number necessary to constitute a formal worship group. We are pleased to present recipes from ten of the choicest Jewish food establishments across the nation. Trust us when we say that they're all worthy of several visits. Enjoy!

D.Z. AKINS
RESTAURANT, DELICATESSEN, BAKERY

6930 Alvarado Road in Alvarado Plaza
San Diego, California 92120
Telephone: (619) 265-0218
Facsimile: (619) 265-8186
Breakfast, Lunch and Dinner
Sunday–Thursday 7:00 am–9:30 pm
Friday & Saturday 7:00 am–11:00 pm
AVERAGE DINNER FOR TWO: $25

ore than seventeen years ago, Debi and Zvika Akin, at that time residents of Los Angeles, decided to pack their bags, move to San Diego and take a stab at cooking for starved delicatessen lovers who constantly reminisced about New York, Chicago, and even Los Angeles.

Although their first date had revolved around a bowl of chopped liver and they both enjoyed cooking, Debi and Zvika had no previous experience in the delicatessen business. But, with their small budget, good old-fashioned recipes, the courage to experiment and work long, hard hours, they opened D. Z. Akins. Their philosophy was simple: "If someone walks into the restaurant and we give them delicious meals, big portions and excellent service at a fair price, they'll be back."

And back they have come—in droves! One doesn't mention the word "delicatessen" in San Diego without following it with "D.Z.'s." Walk into D.Z.'s virtually any hour of the day or evening and you'll see a huge, attractive place packed with animated talkers, eaters, customers—people having a good time in the sense of the old New York-style deli. Besides the restaurant, there's a fully-stocked delicatessen, a bakery with scrumptious goodies, a fountain, and a gift shop filled with Judaica and San Diego souvenirs.

D.Z.'s vast menu (eight pages) contains 103 different sandwiches alone, plus chopped liver, stuffed cabbage, blintzes, borscht and hearty homemade soups. Come to breakfast and enjoy over-generous omelets, bagels, lox and hotcakes.

Sprightly cartoons and signed photographs of famous local T.V. personalities adorn the walls, and the service is always prompt, friendly, and hamish. Small wonder D.Z.'s has won a host of awards through its history, including Best Deli/Restaurant (1996, San Diego Magazine), 1995 Gold Medallion Award for the Best Ethnic Cuisine from the San Diego chapter of the California Restaurant Association, Best Deli by San Diego Magazine (1992, 1993, 1996) and Favorite Ethnic Restaurant and Best Dinner for Two Under $15 in the San Diego Union Night & Day Readers' Poll.

Potato Latkes

4 **large potatoes**
1 **medium onion**
1 **large egg**
 Salt and white pepper
 to taste
½ **cup matzo meal**
 Vegetable oil

rate potatoes and onions (Food processor may be used if desired). Mix with all the other ingredients. Fry in vegetable oil over slow heat until brown. Turn the latkes over and fry for another 5 minutes. Serve with applesauce and/or sour cream. Serves 6 to 8.

Greek Deli Salad

Slice vegetables fine. Mix all ingredients and marinate in the refrigerator overnight. Garnish with parsley.

1 green cabbage
1 green pepper
1 yellow pepper
1 red pepper
1 cucumber, peeled
1 carrot
1 medium red onion
2 stalks celery
1 basket of cherry tomatoes, stems removed
6 oz. Greek olives (Calamatas)
12 oz. herring fillets in wine, drained, cut in small pieces
¾ cup white tarragon vinegar
½ cup vegetable oil or olive oil
Salt and pepper to taste
½ cup sugar to taste

THE BAGEL BAKERY

1132 Forest Avenue
Pacific Grove, California 93950
Telephone: (408) 649-6272

201 Lighthouse
Monterey, California 93940
Telephone: (408) 649-1714

452 Alvarado Street
Monterey, California 93940
Telephone: (408) 372-5242

Carmel Rancho Shopping Center
Carmel, Callifornia 93923
Telephone: (408) 625-5180

969 West Alisal
Salinas, California 93901
Telephone: (408) 758-0280

110 Northridge Shopping Center
Salinas, California 93907
Telephone: (408) 449-1110

Breakfast and Lunch
Open 7 days a week, 6:30 am–6:00 pm
AVERAGE LUNCH FOR TWO: $7.00

When River Gurtin and Bill Leone, two young men who had learned to make bagels in New York the old-fashioned way, started their first Bagel Bakery in 1976, Monterey, California was the last place on earth anyone expected a successful enterprise. There was only a fledgling Jewish community in Monterey at that time, and the bagel craze that swept the '90's was nowhere near a gleam in anyone's eye.

And yet, from Day 1, The Bagel Bakery became a legend—a low-cost place where you could nosh on low-priced, healthy, delicious food, and visit with friends for hours on end. Creative bagel sandwiches soon took their place along such traditional fare as cream cheese and lox on a bagel, and what started out as a place where you could get plain bagels, poppy seed bagels, sesame seed bagels and onion bagels expanded to where, today, you can find more than thirteen varieties of delicious, low-calorie bagels.

And even though River Gurtin has helped start other bagel companies in places as diverse as Los Angeles, Texas, Oregon and Washington, he remains the same modest, unassuming fellow he was when it all started—which is why The Bagel Bakery continues to grow in popularity each year.

Date Nut Cream Cheese

 ombine all ingredients and mix well. Serve on bagel, plain or with lox.

1 lb. cream cheese, softened
2½ oz. dates, chopped
2 oz. walnuts, chopped

★

Vegetable Cream Cheese

5 lbs. cream cheese,
   softened
1 med. onion
½ cup carrots
¼ cup radishes
1 bunch scallions

hop all vegetables well. Blend with cream cheese. Serve on bagels.

Herb Cream Cheese

Mix in ½ oz. herb mix per pound of cream cheese (2½ ounces). Let sit in refrigerator overnight for best flavor.

Herb mix:
- 5 oz. thyme
- 3 oz. garlic powder
- 1 oz. tarragon
- 1 oz. basil powder
- 5 lbs. cream cheese, softened

BAGELSTEIN'S

8104 Spring Valley Road
(Intersection of Spring Valley and Coit)
Dallas, Texas 75240
Telephone: (214) 234-3787
Facsimile: (214) 234-3139
Breakfast, Lunch and Dinner
Tuesday–Saturday: 6:00 am–9:00 pm
Sunday and Monday: 6:00 am–3:00 pm
AVERAGE DINNER FOR TWO: $15

For over 20 years, Bagelstein's has been a Dallas institution—and with good reason. This Kosher style Jewish Deli has full delicatessen, bakery and restaurant facilities. Owner Larry Goldstein, who also serves as President of the Dallas Restaurant Association, has facilities which enable Bagelstein's to cater all kinds of events, both formal and casual, and a banquet room which comfortably holds 70 people. Bagelstein's is conveniently located and easy to get to from anywhere in the Dallas Metroplex. A bright, cheerful meeting place with the ambience you'd expect from a combination of Jewish deli and Texas hospitality, it's a great place to visit when you're in the Lone Star state.

Bagelstein's Noodle Kugel

Mix cream cheese, pineapple chunks with juice, eggs, vanilla extract, sugar and cinnamon well. Place mixture in a greased pan. Press the noodles into the mixture, with most of them remaining on top. Cover with aluminum foil and bake in oven at 350° for one hour. Remove foil and bake for 15 minutes more to brown. Remove from oven. Sprinkle with frosted flakes. Serves 15.

2½ lbs. cream cheese
3 cups pineapple chunks with juice
12 eggs
3 tsps. vanilla extract
1½ cups powdered sugar
¼ tsp. cinnamon
2 cups egg noodles, cooked
6 oz. frosted flakes

★

Bagelstein's Blintzes

Filling:
  3 lbs. cream cheese
  3 lbs. farmer's cheese
  2 tsps. vanilla extract
  ¼ cup lemon juice
  6 eggs
  ½ cup matzo meal
  Blend ingredients well.

Crepes:
  4 cups flour
  2⅔ cups water
  2⅔ cups milk
  ¾ cup melted butter
  12 eggs
  1 tsp. salt

lend flour, water and milk until smooth. Add all other ingredients and mix well. Let stand 30 minutes. Prepare crepe in a 10″ pan. Coat the pan with crepe mixture and let it harden on the bottom. Flip like a pancake and let it brown on the other side. Remove from flame.

After the crepes have cooled, roll 3 ounces of blintz mixture into each crepe. Roll blintz in a cylindrical shape and fry in pan over medium heat until golden brown on both sides.

GLATT DYNASTY
KOSHER CHINESE RESTAURANT

1049 Second Avenue
between 55th and 56th Streets
New York, NY
Telephone: (212) 888-9119
Facsimile: (212) 888-9163
Lunch and Dinner
Sunday: 1:00 pm–11:00 pm
Monday-Thursday: 11:00 am–11:00 pm
Friday: 11:00 am–3:00 pm
Saturday: 1 hour after sunset–1:00 am
AVERAGE DINNER FOR TWO: $45

T he owners of Glatt Dynasty, New York's only Kosher Chinese restaurant, have concentrated their efforts on food, service and ambience. Meticulous attention to detail is evident the moment you walk in the door. The mirrored dining room, which seats fifty, is a sophisticated setting for a business lunch or romantic dinner. Yet, the atmosphere is not so elaborate as to preclude happy family gatherings, and the lovely fish tank at the rear of the restaurant is a colorful diversion and a soothing touch.

Always anxious to ensure the best and most authentic Chinese cuisine, the management frequently visits New York's Chinatown to consult and observe techniques from the Old Country. The needs of health-conscious diners and dieters are met with a full vegetarian menu as well as a diet menu with dishes that are free of salt, sugar, flour or cornstarch.

For those who don't care for Chinese food, Glatt Dynasty offers an American menu featuring steak, American duck, roast chicken and teriyaki steak. All dishes are accompanied by rice: steamed or fried, brown or white.

Glatt Dynasty, which is centrally located across from the Manhattan Art and Antique Center, offers motorcycle delivery (!) throughout Manhattan. All major credit cards are accepted.

Curry Beef

½ lb. lean beef
1 tsp. soy sauce 1 tsp. cornstarch
⅓ tsp. salt
1 tsp. red cooking wine
⅓ tsp. sugar
2 tsps. water, cold
2 tsps. vegetable oil
1 medium onion, with some onion greens
½ tsp. curry powder
2 additional cups of water, cold

ut beef into 1" square thin slices. Place in bowl and marinate with soy sauce, cornstarch, wine, sugar, water and oil for ½ hour. Cut onion into 1" squares.

Sauté and stir-fry the onion. Add curry and stir for ½ minute or so. Add 2 cups of water, salt and sugar. Stir ½ minute more. Add all beef on top. Cook for 15–20 seconds; then stir and mix well. You may deep fry the beef for a few seconds before mixing it in.

Hunan Chicken

C ut chicken into 1" square thin slices. Place in a bowl to marinate with wine, cornstarch, 1 tsp. oil, sugar and water for ½ hour. Deep fry the chicken for a few seconds. Put on the side, ready to use. Heat 1 tsp. oil. Add scallion and sauté for a few seconds. Add all vegetables and stir-fry for about half a minute. Add 2 cups water, salt and sugar. Stir-fry for an additional 30 seconds to 1 minute. Mix well and serve.

Note: You may adjust and create your own taste by adding additional vegetable ingredients of your choice.

½ lb. chicken white meat (boneless and skinless)
2 tsps. wine
1 tsp. cornstarch
½ tsp. salt
¼ tsp. sugar
½ tsp. chopped ginger
2 tsps. cold water
2 tsps. vegetable oil
1 scallion, cut into 1" pieces
Bamboo shoots
Mushrooms
Baby corn
Carrots
Chinese cabbage
Broccoli
Snow pea pods
2 cups cold water

☆

Sautéed Mixed Vegetables

Broccoli
String beans
Water chestnuts
Carrots
Mushrooms
Bok choy
Bamboo shoots
Baby corn
Snow pea pods
⅓ **tsp. salt**
⅓ **tsp. sugar**
2 **tsps. cornstarch**
2 **tsps. water**
2 **cups water**
1 **tsp. vegetable oil**
2 **tsps. soy sauce**

Cut all vegetables about 1" long × ½" wide × ⅛" thick and boil in water for 1–2 minutes, depending on how soft you want the vegetables. Remove from water. Heat oil in a sauce pan. Add all vegetables and stir-fry for 1–2 minutes. Add 2 cups water, salt, sugar and soy sauce. Mix cornstarch and water to make a paste. Bring the mixture in saucepan to a boil. Add cornstarch paste and stir until it has a starchy consistency.

MANNY'S COFFEE SHOP & DELI

1141 S. Jefferson St.
Jefferson St. at Roosevelt Rd.
Chicago, Illinois 60607
Telephone: (312) 939-2855
Facsimile: (312) 939-2856
Breakfast and Lunch
Monday-Saturday, 5:00 am–4:00 pm)
AVERAGE LUNCH FOR TWO: $14

Just a stone's throw from the spot where Mrs. O'Leary's cow kicked over the lamp, sits Chicago's bastion of delicatessen-style bounty. Ken Raskin is the third generation of the Raskins to preside over the rattling of trays and clink of plates at this venerable Chicago institution, which first opened its doors in 1942! In this microcosm of the City of Big Shoulders, the shoulders in the crowded dining rooms belong to aldermen, cops, bookies and traders, moms with their kids just over from shoe-shopping at Chernin's, neighborhood folks and schmatta salesmen. Latkes, kishke and knishes are not the only delicacies filling those trays. A goodly portion of the Raskins' diners take all their meals at Manny's. The extensive menu provides a wide range of choices—from hearty beef stew to generous fruit plates. Even if the dining room weren't such an interesting place to people watch, the food alone is worth the trip.

Manny's Famous Chicken Soup With Matzo Balls

Chicken Broth:
- 1 **chicken (4–5 lbs.)**
- 4 **qts. Cold water**
- 1 **medium onion**
- 2 **whole carrots**
- 1 **clove garlic**
  Leaves and bottom of
  2 celery bunches
- ½ **oz. parsley leaves**
- 1 **Tbsp. salt**
- ½ **tsp. pepper**

Place cut-up chicken in pot of cold water. Cover and bring to boil. Add all ingredients and simmer for 3 hours. Strain and skim fat from top.

Matzo Balls (Knaidelach)

Combine the eggs, fat, matzo meal and beat well. Add water and salt to make a stiff batter. Cover and chill in refrigerator for 2 hours. Wet hand with cold water to prevent sticking. Form batter into small balls and drop into boiling water. Allow to boil for 30 minutes. Drain and serve in chicken broth.

1 cup matzo meal
¼ cup chicken fat or shortening
1 tsp. salt
2 eggs
¼–½ cup water

Potato Pancakes (Latkes)

10 medium potatoes
1 medium to large onion
3 eggs, beaten
3 Tbsps. flour
1 tsp. salt
¼ tsp. pepper

Grate potatoes and allow to sit for 10 minutes. Remove water and discard. Grate onion. Stir all ingredients together. Use immediately. Heat pan filled to ½ inch deep with shortening. When shortening is hot, spoon batter into pan to desired size. Brown on both sides, turning only once.

MILLER'S DELICATESSEN

2849 Smith Avenue
Baltimore, Maryland 21209
Telephone: (410) 358-3222
Facsimile: (410) 602-2254
Breakfast, Lunch and Dinner
Open 7 days a week: 6:00 am 9:00 pm
AVERAGE DINNER FOR TWO: $15

After 27 years as a popular gathering place on Reisterstown Road, the old wood paneled New York-style deli has moved to its gleaming new Art-Deco, high-tech home on Smith Avenue in the middle of Jewish Baltimore. Now expanded to 4,500 square feet of space, including a 100-seat capacity restaurant and a full-service delicatessen, owner Larry Abel, who's been with Miller's since 1967, has not changed his style of "Give the customers what they like best—and give it from your heart!"

Miller's Deli caters party platters. The establishment is particularly noted for its corned beef-cole slaw-Russian dressing sandwiches, its stuffed cabbage, noodle kugel, and the feeling of ambience and hamishkeit that has made it a Baltimore landmark.

Mushroom Barley Soup

8 cups water
6 oz. package barley
1 cup carrots, diced
1 cup celery, chopped
1 whole onion, chopped
2 cups mushrooms, stems and pieces
1 cup chopped beef flanken (flank steak)
Salt and pepper to taste

n a large pot, add water with all ingredients. Simmer for 1½ hours, stirring occasionally.

☆

Miller's Signature Stuffed Cabbage

Boil cabbage until core gets soft. Separate leaves. Peel off the cabbage leaves. Mix chopped meat, rice, salt, pepper and green pepper together. Add raisins (optional).

Place ¼ lb. (ice cream dipper) of meat mixture in each cabbage leaf and roll tight, setting in pan.

Sauce: Mix tomato sauce, water, lemon juice, brown and white sugar together. Cook for 1 hour.

Pour over rolled cabbage, place in baking dish and bake for 1½ hours at 350°

1 large head of cabbage
1 lb ground beef, chopped
¼ cup uncooked white rice
½ tsp. salt
¼ tsp. pepper
½ tsp. green pepper, chopped
1 can tomato sauce
1 can water
2 tsps. lemon juice
4 Tbsps. brown sugar
1 Tbsp. white sugar
½ cup raisins (optional)

Meat Knishes

3 lb. roast beef
 (fresh brisket)
2 onions
 Salt and pepper to taste
 Garlic

Dough:
 1 cup flour
 1 tsp. baking powder
 3 eggs
 ¼ tsp. salt
 ¼ cup vegetable oil
 ½ tsp. egg whites

Egg Wash:
 4 egg yolks
 ¼ cup water

ut roast beef in pot and boil for 3 hours, until meat gets soft and falls apart. Grind or finely chop the beef and remaining ingredients together.

Dough:

Place all ingredients in mixing bowl and mix dough. Roll dough with rolling pin until about ⅛″ thick. Cut dough into 3″x3″ squares. Put 1 Tbsp. of the meat mixture in the center of each square and fold over, covering the mixture. Hand shape into balls. Flatten bottoms of each ball by gently pressing against wooden board. Pour egg wash (See ingredients below) over the knishes.

Egg Wash:

Place knishes on baking pan and bake at 350° for ½ hour or until golden brown.

PUMPERNICKLE'S REAL DELI

1036 Olive Street Road
(Creve Coeur–West County Suburb)
St. Louis, Missouri 63141
Telephone: (314) 567-4496
Facsimile: (314) 567-3257
Breakfast and Lunch
Tuesday-Friday, 6:30 am–2:30 pm
Saturday and Sunday, 7:00 am–2:30 pm
Deli: Tuesday-Friday, 6:30 am-5:00 pm
Saturday, 7:00 am–5:00 pm
Sunday, 7:00 am–3:30 pm
AVERAGE LUNCH FOR TWO: $15

PUMPERNICKLE'S REAL DELI started life over 20 years ago as Tel Aviv Deli. It occupied a single suburban storefront and consisted of a couple of refrigerated cases, a bakery case and two tiny tables. In 1994, Tel Aviv changed hands, modernized, and became PUMPERNICKLE'S. Its new incarnation finds it in two unassuming, but attractive, storefronts which barely hint at the huge and varied selection of choice foods to be found inside. Customers will find deli cases full of the traditional smoked fish, meats, salads and desserts to take out, and a 60-seat restaurant where breakfast and lunch is served.

Owner/chefs Brad Hartman and Rob Hodes are not what you would expect to find behind the counter and grill of a deli. Both are classically trained Culinary Institute of America graduates. They left the world of fine dining to apply their considerable talents to the world of deli.

Their "real Deli" concept borrows from the traditions of New York and Chicago, adds a little Midwestern homeyness, and serves it all up with a chef's flair. But don't expect abuse of tradition here. The matzo ball soup is a tribute to Jewish grandmothers everywhere: rich, golden and redolent of chicken and carrot. Baked items are made the old-fashioned way. The rugelach, komish bread, cheesecakes and apple strudels taste good enough to make even the most discriminating "bubbie" happy. Knishes are a hand-made specialty. These huge, softball-sized pastries come in 5 choices, from the traditional kasha, meat or potato, to the more modern spinach, broccoli or cheddar. Smoked fish is flown in twice a week from New York and Florida, and PUMPERNICKLE'S deli cases boast one of the best selections available in the Midwest.

An extensive catering menu offers everything from hot dinners to long sandwiches, deli, dairy and fish platters, to dessert trays. For sit-down dining, take-home deli and party catering, you'll hunt a long way to find such great food in the Midwest.

Komish or "Mandel" Bread

5 eggs, whole
1½ cups sugar, granulated
1½ cups salad oil
2 tsps. vanilla extract
1½ cups pecans, chopped
12 oz. (1 pkg.) chocolate
chips
1½ lbs. flour, bread

To dust:
½ cup sugar, granulated
1 Tbsp. cocoa powder

Place first 5 ingredients in mixer with dough hook or paddle. Mix 1 minute, add flour, and mix another minute. Or, if by hand, mix first 4 ingredients with a wooden spoon or spatula until sugar is dissolved, 1 minute, add pecans and chocolate chips and mix well. Add flour and mix 1–2 minutes, or until well incorporated.

Brush an 11"×17" shallow baking pan with salad oil. Place dough in middle and spread evenly into pan. Smooth the top as well as possible with an oiled knife. Make slashes all the way through the dough, cutting it into 1"×2" pieces. This will make cutting much easier after baking. Mix the last of the sugar and cocoa powder. Sprinkle evenly over the top.

Bake at 300° on middle rack for 30–40 minutes. The Komish will be puffed evenly and firm to the touch. Remove from the oven and allow to cool, 4–5 minutes. Run the knife back through the cuts you made earlier, making sure to cut to pan. Cool.

Traditionally, Komish is aged, uncovered, for 3 or 4 days and toasted for 20 minutes in a 325° oven to crisp, then served at room temperature. Served untoasted, they will more closely resemble a good shortbread.

Komish is the St. Louis name for what is traditionally known as Mandel Bread. In the tradition of biscotti, it is usually left to age, then toasted until crisp, and served with coffee for dunking. This version is a modern adaptation, using pecans instead of the more traditional walnuts, and adding chocolate chips, which give the cookies a sweeter edge. These fall somewhere between a shortbread and a biscotti, and make a great snack or light dessert with ice cream and coffee. Komish will stay good at room temperature for a month or so, and can be frozen indefinitely.

Chopped Liver

This delicious recipe comes in two parts, the liver and the garnish. It is best made a day before you plan to serve it as the flavors develop when they sit. We cook and grind the liver one day, then mix in the garnish and serve it the next. We suggest that you use a meat grinder to chop the liver. A food processor will work as well, although the texture will be a bit fine for our tastes. The recipe yields 15 servings. Too much? Hey, this is Jewish food! We always cook for a crowd! The recipe can easily be halved for smaller get-togethers.

Rinse chicken and beef livers under cold, running water, removing outer skin. Place them in a pot with enough cold water to cover. Bring to a boil, turn down, and simmer for 15 minutes. The liver will be evenly pink/white throughout. Strain, discarding the cooking liquid. Cool.

While the livers are simmering, rough chop the onion, place in a pan with the oil, and roast over medium high heat, stirring frequently until dark, golden brown. Cool.

Mix livers, onions and eggs together and run through a meat grinder with medium disk, or mix the liver and onions, place in a food processor and chop with quick pulses until a rough paste. Process the eggs separately. Mix the two together. Refrigerate for a few hours or overnight.

Add garnish ingredients to the liver. Mix well.

Liver:
- 2½ lbs. chicken liver
- 1¼ lb. beef liver
- 3 large yellow onions
- 1 cup salad oil
- 7 eggs, hard-boiled

Garnish:
- 1 cup yellow onion, diced fine
- ½ cup salad oil
- 7 eggs, hard-boiled, roughly chopped
- ¼ tsp. black pepper or to taste
- 1 tsp. salt or to taste

☆

RAJBHOG

738 Adams Avenue
(at Tabor)
Philadelphia, PA 19124
Telephone: (215) 537-1937
Lunch and Dinner
Tuesday–Sunday, 11:00 am–10:00 pm
Closed Mondays
AVERAGE DINNER FOR TWO: $25

From the center of the city take Route #76 West, then exit for Route #1 North Roosevelt Blvd. Stay in the center lanes of Route #1. Exit at Adams Avenue. Pass two lights and make a left behind McDonald's. Enter Adams & Tabor Shopping Center and look for RAJBHOG next to Baskin & Robbins Ice Cream store. If this sounds like a bit of cloak and dagger stuff—perhaps a bit sinister—let this be a lesson that you should never judge a restaurant by its location. RAJBHOG is located in Northeast Philadelphia in a slightly run-down strip mall, half hidden by a fast food emporium off the boulevard.

Once you enter, however, you're in a different world as you inhale the aphrodisiac aroma of toasted cumin and coriander. The family that operates RAJBHOG—the only Kosher-certified Indian restaurant we were able to find in the Northeast (if not the nation)—specializes in vegetarian cuisine from the Gujarati region of India. This cuisine is typified by carefully prepared and finely chopped ingredients and a light hand with spices and oils. If you often find Indian food too heavy or too highly flavored, you will fall in love with RAJBHOG.

RAJBHOG offers a large variety of entrées and side dishes at very reasonable prices, or you can choose from four different combination platters called "Thalis." All food is freshly prepared from scratch on the premises. Each Sunday, from 5:00 pm to 9:00 pm, RAJBHOG features an Indian festival—all-you-can-eat buffet for a very reasonable price per person.

This wonderful restaurant is certainly a "find"—a hidden treasure to be savored time and time again.

Bombay Style Potato Curry

Scrub and wash potatoes, leaving the skin on. Cut unpeeled potatoes into 1" cubes. Heat vegetable oil in a large skillet. Add cumin seed, ginger, garlic and green chiles and fry for 3 minutes. Add potatoes and 4 cups of water when potatoes are almost cooked. Add 1 cup yogurt (Dahi), turmeric, salt and sugar or honey. Keep on low flame. When you see that the curry is getting thicker, remove from stove and add chopped coriander. Serve hot or at room temperature. Serves 6–8.

4–5 medium potatoes
2 Tbsps. vegetable oil
1 cup yogurt (Dahi)
½ tsp. cumin seed
1 tsp. chopped ginger
½ tsp. chopped garlic
¼ tsp. chopped green chiles, or to taste
½ tsp. turmeric powder
Salt to taste
1 Tbsp. sugar or honey
2 Tbsps. fresh coriander, chopped

Toor Dal with Spinach

1½ cups uncooked toor dal
1½ cups chopped spinach
 1 med. onion, chopped
 1 tsp. cumin seed
 ½ tsp. turmeric powder
 1 med. tomato, chopped
 ¼ cup whole peanuts
 1 tsp. lemon juice
 4 cloves garlic, chopped
 ¼ tsp. chile powder, or to taste
 3 Tbsps. corn oil
 1 tsp. grated ginger
   Salt to taste

I n a separate pot, cook toor dal with 4 cups of water, about 20–25 minutes. Rinse spinach leaves in several changes of water until all the sand is washed away, then chop 1½ cups of spinach. Heat oil in a large skillet over high temperature. Add cumin, onion, garlic and ginger and fry for at least 2 minutes. Combine cooked toor dal with spinach, turmeric powder, tomato, lemon juice, whole peanuts and salt in the pot containing the water and toor dal. Bring to boil. Continue cooking over low-to-medium heat for 10–15 minutes. Serve hot with rice. Serves 6–8.

Moongdal Wada

C lean and wash yellow dal and flour and soak in water for 4 hours. Grind the yellow dal mixture coarsely. Add chopped chile peppers, ginger, chopped coriander, salt, garlic and cumin seed. Stir all ingredients except oil for frying. Mix well.

Heat oil in a deep fryer until it is very hot. Shape above mixture into 1″ balls (about 1 heaping Tbsp. for each ball) and add each ball slowly to the hot oil fryer. Cook for about 4 minutes on the first side. Turn and fry the other side, about 3 minutes. Drain on paper towel and serve. Serves 6–8.

- 3 cups yellow grain dal
- ½ cup grain flour
- ½ tsp. green chile peppers, to taste
- 1 tsp. ginger, chopped
- ½ tsp. cumin seed
- 3 Tbsps. fresh coriander, chopped
  Salt to taste
  Vegetable oil

STAGE DELI

834 7th Avenue
Manhattan
New York, N.Y. 10019
Telephone: (212) 245-7850
Facsimile: (212) 245-7957
Breakfast, Lunch and Dinner
Open 7 days a week, 6:00 am–2:00 am
AVERAGE DINNER FOR TWO: $25-$30

E very delicatessen in America likes to claim it is a "New York-style deli." It's like "playing the Palace." And yet, when one thinks of the New York Deli par excellence, only one name springs instantly to mind: The Stage Deli. Situated in the dead center of New York's Great White Way—Broadway—the Theater District—The Stage Deli has been saucily serving the most famous stars of stage and screen, and all manner of not-so-famous folk, since 1937. In sixty years, there have been many changes on the New York scene, but one thing has remained constant: You can get great food at a reasonable price at the Stage.

Signed pictures of celebrities dot the well-worn walls, the hot corned beef sandwiches are lean, the pastrami tasty, and rich tastes and aromas surround you in every section. There are many "Stage" Delis in many cities throughout the United States, but this one's the one!

Chicken Soup

I n a 3 quart pot, bring water, onions, celery and dill to a boil. Add chicken, either whole or in quarters. Simmer for approximately 2 hours. Salt and pepper to taste. Skim the fat off the top. Purée carrots and add them to the soup. Add noodles, optional.

1 **pullet, cooking chicken**
¾ **cup water**
2 **large Spanish onions, cut in half**
   Salt and pepper to taste.
3 **stalks celery, cut**
1 **bunch dill**
3 **large carrots, peeled**
   Noodles (optional)

☆

Chopped Liver

2½ lbs. chicken liver
3 large Spanish onions
8 eggs, hard boiled
  Salt
  Pepper
  Garlic powder

Sauté chicken liver and onions together. Cook until liver is fully cooked through, then add hard boiled eggs, chopped. Put liver, onions and eggs into either a blender or mixer, something that will smooth out the mixture, adding salt, pepper and garlic. Garnish with white radish, lettuce and tomato. Serves 10.

☆

Tabouli's Mediterranean Delicatessen & Cafe

309 Lighthouse Avenue
Monterey, California 93940
Telephone: (408) 646-0319
Lunch and Dinner
Monday through Saturday, 11:00 a.m.–7:15p.m.
AVERAGE MEAL FOR TWO: $20

At any given time, there are over 350 restaurants in the greater Monterey—Carmel tourist area. So why would both locals and the international community from the Defense Language Institute and the U.S. Naval Postgraduate School flock each noon to a tiny (16 seat) deli-restaurant on one of the city's busiest thoroughfares?

The answer is simple: Tabouli's gives extraordinary value for the money—outstanding, genuine, homemade Middle Eastern cuisine at a price that's hard to beat! Chef Christophe, owner of Monterey's highly reputed Christophe's Bakery as well as Tabouli's, has not only been a private chef in Pebble Beach, but has also served in places as diverse as Beirut, Paris and nearby Carmel.

At Tabouli's, he proudly serves foods from Bulgaria, Egypt, France, Greece, Hungary, Israel, Italy and Turkey, as well as from his native Lebanon. The pride shows as he treats each customer as an individual, showing pictures of his family—and gorgeous photographs of the meals he has produced—and suggesting—but never forcing—that the patron take interesting chances on new tastes and textures.

Chef Christophe has given us two very special recipes for this book: If any of you have ever visited Israel, the most popular meals you will find anywhere in the country are falafel (ground, fried chickpeas) and shawerma (shaved meat) served in pita bread with tahini dressing.

So it is fitting that the final dishes in the "Professionals" section take us out of the United States to the land of Eretz Israel—the State of Israel.

Falafel

3 cups garbanzo beans (chickpeas), soaked at least 5–6 hours in hot water or overnight in cold water
1 large onion
6 cloves garlic
2 Tbsps. coriander
2 Tbsps. cumin, ground
2 tsps. flour
1 cup water
2 tsps. Allspice
1½ tsps. salt
1 Tbsp. baking powder
Corn oil for cooking

Garnish:
Shredded lettuce
Sliced tomato
Tahini sauce

Tahini sauce:
½ cup sesame seed tahini (You can purchase this from Tabouli's)
½ cup lemon juice
½ cup water
1 tsp. salt
7 cloves garlic

Mix garlic and onion in food processor for 1 minute. Add garbanzo beans and mash for 2 more minutes, until fine. Add water and blend for another minute. Add coriander, cumin, flour, allspice and salt and mix for one final minute.

Prepare skillet or deep fryer by filling half full with corn oil (do not use olive oil) and heat. The oil must be very hot—at least 375° or the falafel will fall apart.

Just before shaping, add baking powder to the mixture. Do not use soda, which will cause the balls to turn dark gray instead of golden brown. Shape the mixture into walnut-sized balls and drop into hot oil. Fry until the first side turns golden brown—about 1½ minutes. Turn and fry until the other side turns golden brown—another 1 to 1½ minutes.

Serve in pita bread (pocket bread), garnished with shredded lettuce, sliced tomato and tahini sauce (See recipe below).

Tahini sauce:

Mix garlic and salt in food processor. Add tahini and blend for 30 seconds. Add lemon juice and water and blend for an additional 30 seconds. The consistency should be creamy and soft, like a topping or sauce. If too thick, add water.

This may be served on top of the falafel or served in a small cup next to the pita (pocket bread) for dipping.

Shawerma

Slice meat very thin and cut into strips such as breakfast beef, fajitas or jerky. Mix all ingredients except tomatoes in a baking dish or shallow pan. Cover and let sit overnight.

Next day, add 3 tomatoes, sliced in half, to the top of the meat. Roast in 350° oven for 1 hour.

Serve in pita (pocket bread), accompanied by shredded lettuce, sliced tomatoes and tahini or hummus.

2 lbs. boneless lamb or 2 lbs. lean beef, sliced very thin (¼" thick)
3 Tbsps. allspice
3 large onions, sliced thin
1 tsp. cardamom, ground
1 tsp. salt, or to taste
1 cup corn oil
½ cup vinegar
3 tomatoes

Garnish:
Shredded lettuce
Sliced tomatoes
Tahini sauce or
hummus

(This meal is famous throughout the Near and Middle East where it goes by many names, as well as by the Israeli name, Shawerma. In any language, it is mouth watering and delicious).

☆

Marvin Shapiro's Favorite Recipes

Who (or what) Is Marvin Shapiro???

Funny you should ask. Finally, we have corralled someone that no other cookbook has ever featured!

It is a little-known, but genuine, fact that MARVIN SHAPIRO, world-famed (at least in his own mind) trial lawyer, raconteur, bon vivant and author of the renowned HOW TO SUR-VIVE—AND PROFIT FROM—YOUR SON'S BAR MITZVAH (Wachtman Books, $9.95) and HOW TO SURVIVE—AND PROFIT FROM—YOUR DAUGHTER'S BAT MITZVAH (Wachtman Books, $9.95) was, for the first twenty-five years of his life, a "Deli Man."

Yep, old Marv grew up on Pico Boulevard in West Los Angeles (Picwood Delicatessen) until his late father moved to North Hollywood (Freddie's Delicatessen) and subsequently to the Western-Manchester section of Los Angeles (Freddie's BEST Delicatessen), and while he for-sook the food business 'til now, he has graciously (and at no cost to us) consented to give us a few of his choicest recipes.

So . . . here's MARVIN!

Marvin's Roast Brisket

**Fresh brisket of beef
(about 4–5 lbs.)**
1 **packet dried onion
soup mix**
1 **can tomato sauce
(16 oz.)**
1 **tsp. ginger**
½ **tsp. salt**
⅓ **cup red wine**
2 **medium onions, sliced**
2 **tsps. garlic powder
(Optional)**

I nto a large measuring cup pour onion soup mix, tomato sauce, ginger, salt, wine, and, if desired, garlic powder. Mix well. Place brisket on large sheet of heavy duty aluminum foil. Smother brisket with sauce and top with sliced onion. Wrap the brisket well, so that the sauce won't leak out. You may wish to use another large sheet of heavy duty aluminum foil and wrap the brisket crosswise. Place package in roasting pan. Roast in 325° oven for 2½ hours. Unwrap brisket, making sure you don't lose the sauce. Slice and place on serving dish. Pour ½ of the sauce over the meat. Pour the rest into a gravy bowl and serve alongside the brisket. This is especially delicious served with boiled new potatoes.

Marvin's Barbecued Salmon (Which is a lot cheaper than lox!)

Place fish on large piece of heavy-duty aluminum foil (enough to totally wrap the fish). Liberally rub bay leaves, dill weed, sliced onion, butter, margarine or olive oil, cooking wine, lemon juice and garlic powder into cavity of fish. Pour tomato sauce on both sides of the fish and wrap fish completely in foil.

Broil aluminum-wrapped fish for 20 minutes on each side. During the last 5 minutes, you might want to unwrap the foil to allow for added crispness.

1 whole salmon, king or sockeye, (4–5 lbs.), head and tail removed
2 bay leaves
1 Tbsp. dill weed
1 medium onion
1 tsp. butter, margarine or olive oil
2 Tbsps. red cooking wine
1 tsp. lemon juice
1 tsp. garlic powder
1 can tomato sauce (8 oz.)

Marvin's Simple Roast Chicken

1 **3–4 lb. frying chicken (or 4–5 lb. roaster)**

1 **green apple, quartered**

1 **medium onion, quartered**

1 **tsp. ground ginger**

1 **tsp. garlic powder**

1 **tsp. onion powder**

1 **tsp. paprika**

Clean out chicken, removing neck, heart, liver and gizzards. Fill the cavity with apple, onion, ginger, garlic powder and onion powder. Sprinkle paprika on top. Set in roasting pan, covered with aluminum foil and roast in 350° oven for 1½ hours. Remove foil and roast for an additional 20–30 minutes or until skin is crisp and golden brown. Serves 6 normal people or 3 fressers.

Marvin's Genuine Delicatessen Cole Slaw

S hred or slice the cabbage. Add grated carrots, vinegar, celery seed. Mix the ingredients by hand, slowly adding sugar and mayonnaise until you get a taste that's sweet-tart and a consistency that's creamy, but not too thick. Serves 6.

2 medium heads green cabbage, cored
2 carrots, grated
½ cup vinegar
2 Tbsps. celery seed
Sugar to taste
1–2 cups mayonnaise, to taste

★

Marvin's Luau Chicken Roast
(Aloha Oy! This one you'll enjoy!)

1 whole fryer-broiler
 chicken (3–4 lbs.)
1 tsp. garlic powder or
 1 clove garlic
1 tsp. salt
1 tsp. ginger or 3 thin
 slices ginger root
1 small apple
2 small onions
3 carrots
2 yams or sweet potatoes
2 medium potatoes,
 peeled
1 or 2 sprigs broccoli
 (optional)
1 tsp. paprika
2 Tbsps. honey

Clean cavity of chicken, removing heart, liver, neck and gizzards. Fill the cavity with garlic or garlic powder, salt and ginger. Quarter the apple and one of the onions and stuff into cavity. Place chicken in a large baking dish. Cut carrots, potatoes and yams in quarters and surround the chicken with these vegetables and with the broccoli. Sprinkle paprika over the chicken. Spoon the honey over the chicken. Cover the dish with aluminum foil and place in 350° oven for 1 hour. Remove foil. Roast for another ½ hour or until brown.

Makes four generous servings.

Marvin's Genuine Delicatessen Potato Salad

Cut the potatoes into chunks. Add celery, cut into ½" pieces, plus eggs, onion, mustard and mayonnaise. Mix by hand. Add sugar, salt and pepper to taste. You may wish to add more mayonnaise for a creamier consistency.

6 **potatoes, boiled and cooled**
2 **celery stalks**
2 **eggs, hard-boiled**
1 **large onion, sliced thin**
2 **Tbsps. mustard**
2 **Tbsps. mayonnaise**
   Sugar, salt and pepper to taste

Maui Broiled Ahi Tuna

4 filets Ahi tuna, about
½ to ¾" thick
3 Tbsps. soy sauce or
teriyaki sauce
1 tsp. powdered ginger
1 Tbsp. mustard
1–2 onions

Combine soy sauce, powdered ginger and mustard to make marinade. Soak tuna filets in marinade for 5 minutes. Slice onions very thinly. Place half of the onion slices over marinaded tuna and place on broiling pan or foil in oven set to broil. Broil for 5 minutes. Turn. Place the other half of the onion slices on top of the tuna and broil for 5 minutes more. You may shorten the time to 3 minutes on each side if desired, since most Hawaiian chefs serve Ahi seared on the outside, very rare on the inside. Serves four.

☆

How You Can Measure Up . . .

LIQUID MEASURES

1 dash	3 to 6 drops
1 teaspoon (tsp.)	⅓ tablespoon
1 tablespoon (Tbsp.)	3 teaspoons
1 tablespoon	½ fluid ounce
1 fluid ounce	2 tablespoons
1 cup	½ pint
1 cup	16 tablespoons
1 cup	8 fluid ounces
1 pint	2 cups
1 pint	16 fluid ounces

DRY MEASURES

1 pinch	less than ⅛ teaspoon
1 teaspoon	⅓ tablespoon
1 tablespoon	3 teaspoons
¼ cup	4 tablespoons
⅓ cup	5 tablespoons plus 1 teaspoon
½ cup	8 tablespoons
⅔ cup	10 tablespoons plus 2 teaspoons
¾ cup	12 tablespoons
1 cup	16 tablespoons

VEGETABLES AND FRUITS

Apple (1 medium)	1 cup chopped
Avocado (1 medium)	1 cup mashed
Broccoli (1 stalk)	2 cups florets
Cabbage (1 large)	10 cups, chopped
Carrot (1 medium)	½ cup, diced
Celery (3 stalks)	1 cup, diced
Eggplant (1 medium)	4 cups, cubed
Lemon (1 medium)	2 tablespoons juice
Onion (1 medium)	1 cup diced
Orange (1 medium)	½ cup juice
Parsley (1 bunch)	3 cups, chopped
Spinach (fresh), 12 cups, loosely packed	1 cup cooked
Tomato (1 medium)	¾ cup, diced
Zucchini (1 medium)	2 cups, diced

APPROXIMATE EQUIVALENTS

1 stick butter = ½ cup = 8 Tbsps. = 4 oz.
1 cup all-purpose flour = 5 oz.
1 cup cornmeal (polenta) = 4½ oz.
1 cup sugar = 8 oz.
1 cup powdered sugar = 4½ oz.
1 cup brown sugar = 6 oz.
1 large egg = 2 oz. = ¼ cup = 4 Tbsps.
1 egg yolk = 1 Tbsp. + 1 tsp.
1 egg white = 2 Tbsps. + 2 tsps.

Metric Conversion Chart

CONVERSIONS TO OUNCES TO GRAMS

To convert ounces to grams, multiply number of ounces by 28.35.

1 oz. . . . . . 30 g.	6 oz. . . . . 180 g.	11 oz. . . . 300 g.	16 oz. . . . 450 g.
2 oz. . . . . . 60 g.	7 oz. . . . . 200 g.	12 oz. . . . 340 g.	20 oz. . . . 570 g.
3 oz. . . . . . 85 g.	8 oz. . . . . 225 g.	13 oz. . . . 370 g.	24 oz. . . . 680 g.
4 oz. . . . . 115 g.	9 oz. . . . . 250 g.	14 oz. . . . 400 g.	28 oz. . . . 790 g.
5 oz. . . . . 140 g.	10 oz. . . . 285 g.	15 oz. . . . 425 g.	32 oz. . . . 900 g.

CONVERSIONS OF QUARTS TO LITERS

To convert quarts to liters, multiply number of quarts by 0.95.

1 qt. . . . . . . 1 L	2 ½ qt. . . . . 2½ L	5 qt. . . . . . 4¾ L	8 qt. . . . . . 7½ L
1½ qt. . . . . 1½ L	3 qt. . . . . . 2¾ L	6 qt. . . . . . 5½ L	9 qt. . . . . . 8½ L
2 qt. . . . . . . 2 L	4 qt. . . . . . 3¾ L	7 qt. . . . . . 6½ L	10 qt. . . . . 9½ L

CONVERSION OF FAHRENHEIT TO CELSIUS

To convert **Fahrenheit to Celsius**, subtract 32 from the Fahrenheit figure,
multiply by 5, then divide by 9.

OTHER CONVERSIONS

To convert **ounces to milliliters**, multiply number of ounces by 30.
To convert **cups to liters**, multiply number of cups by 0.24.
To convert **inches to centimeters**, multiply number of inches by 2.54.

List Of Contributors To The Original Congregation Beth Isreal Cookbook, "Jewish Cooking From Here And Far"

Deanna Adolph
Joyce Kurtz
Ethel Alvey
Judy Levine
Amos Amit
Barbara Lewit
Siglinde Applebaum
Trudy Licht
Charles Beren
Barbara Lipman
Kerry Beren
Heather Mendel
Dennis Bates
Rabbi Norman Mendel
Gail Bates
Ilona Milch
Beverly G. Bean
Barbara Mitchell
Charles Blum
Beverly Movson
Ettie Buch
Margye Neswitz
Martha Casanave
Beny Neta
Terri Chaplan
Tamar Neta
Maureen Chodosh
Ann Packer
Maria Gitin-Cozzini
Katherine Penebre
Andrea Carter
Stuart Pressman

Cathleen Connell
Barbara Quinn
Barbara Daily
Ronnie Ramistella
Sharon Delsohn
Judy Reibel
Mrs. Paul Dublin
Norma Robinson
Meryl Peters-Ehrlich
Jo Anne Rockower
Sonja Ehrlich
Regina "Ginny" Rosenberg
Joyce Fischbein
Betsy Rosenthal
Hugo Gerstl
Diana Rosenthal
Lorraine Gerstl
Neal Rosenthal
Carol Gilbert
Rick Rosenthal
Shelly Glaser
Natalie Sammett
Freda Golding
Anna Shelkowsky
Susan Gorelick
Anita Silver
Rabbi Bruce Greenbaum
Deborah Smolen
Susan Greenbaum
Lynne Sneiderman
Carol Gross
Larry Solow

Rabbi Mark Gross
Zane Speiser
Lucille Hallisey
Esther Stern
Elaine Halprin
Maxine Suval
Malka Hanna
Barbara Taylor
Jinx Havas
Cath Tendler
Ty Havas
Lester Tockerman
Linda Kaiser
Phyllis Torin
Rick Kaiser
Lillian Ullman
Connie Kean
Betty Unger
Shelli Klein
Jeannine Ushana
Adeline Kohn
Zelma Weinfield
Ellen Krause
Mimi Weingarten
Eda Kunitz
Bonny Weinstein
Beth Weissman
Marta Weltsch
Karen Wiskoff

Recipe Index

*(*Denotes delicatessen or restaurant recipes)*
*(**Denotes Marvin Shapiro's favorite recipes)*

Selected Glossary of Jewish Terms

BAGEL. A bread roll made of yeast dough and shaped like a dougnut.

BAR MITZVAH. The ceremony for a boy reaching religious maturity (13).

BAT MITZVAH. The ceremony for a girl reaching religious maturity.

B.C.E. Before the common era, i.e. B.C.

BIMAH. The reading dais in the center of the synagogue.

BLINTZES. Very thin rolled pancakes, filled with cheese, fruit or meat.

CHALLAH. Sabbath or holiday twists of white egg bread.

CHANUKAH. Literally dedication. The Festival of Lights.

CHAROSET. A mixture of chopped apples and nuts seasoned with cinnamon and wine–a Passover Seder symbol.

CHOLENT. A Sabbath oven dish prepared on Friday and cooked overnight in a very slow oven.

CHUPPAH. The wedding canopy.

DAYS OF AWE. The High Holy Days, beginning with Rosh Hashanah and ending with Yom Kippur. Usually observed during September or early October.

DREIDEL. A four-sided spinning top spun by children during the festival of Chanukah.

ETROG. Citron fruit used with the festive bouquet on Sukkot.

FARFEL. Noodle dough, grated or chopped into barley-sized grains.

GALUPTZE. Stuffed cabbage or grape leaves (Russian).

GEFILTE FISH. Stuffed fish.

HAGGADAH. The book of the Seder, giving the story, meaning and written order of the Passover ceremony.

HAMANTASCHEN. Three-cornered cakes filled with poppy seed or prune filling. Traditional for Purim.

KASHA. Literally, a mush from any cereal. Today it means buckwheat groats.

KOSHER. According to Jewish dietary laws.

KIDDUSH. The prayer of sanctification of the Sabbath or of a holiday, recited over wine.

KNAIDELACH. Dumplings.

KNISHES. Patties or dumplings stuffed with potato mixture, meat mixture or kasha.

KREPLACH. Noodle dough cut round or square and filled with cheese or meat.

KUCHEN. Assorted coffee cakes.

KUGEL. Pudding.

LATKES. Potato pancakes.

LOX. Smoked salmon.

LUKSHEN. Noodles.

LULAV. The ceremonial bouquet of willow, myrtle and palm branches used during Sukkot.

MATZO. Unleavened bread eaten during Passover.

MENORAH. Candelabra.

MITZVAH. A good deed.

MOHN. Poppy seed.

MANDELBROT. A special variety of almond-flavored pastry.

MINYAN. Ten—the minimum number of Jews (traditionally Jewish males) needed in order to conduct a formal prayer service.

PAREVE. (pronounced par' vey): Applies to foods such as fish, eggs, fruit and vegetables that can be eaten with either meat or milk dishes (i.e. neutral).

PASSOVER OR PESACH. The holiday that commemorates the Exodus of the Israelites from Egypt.

PURIM. The historical festival that celebrates the Biblical Book of Esther.

RABBI. Literally, my master. An ordained teacher of Jewish law, authorized to decide questions of law and ritual; the spiritual head of a congregation.

ROSH HASHANAH. "Head" of the year; new year. First of the High Holy Days.

SCHAV. Sorrel grass or spinach soup.

SCHMALTZ. Literally, fat. Rendered fats of meat and poultry.

SCHOCHET. A man trained and authorized to slaughter animals and fowl in accordance with Jewish dietary laws.

SHABBAT. Sabbath, the Day of Rest. From sundown Friday to sundown Saturday.

SHAVUOT. The Feast of Weeks.

SHOFAR. Trumpet made from a ram's horn. It is blown on the High Holy Days.

SIMCHAT TORAH. Important festival celebrating the giving of the Torah.

SUKKOT. The festival of booths, also known as the Feast of Tabernacles, celebrating the end of the summer harvest.

TALLIT. Prayer shawl worn by Jews.

TALMUD. Collection of writings containing Jewish civil and religious laws.

TEIGLACH. Small balls of dough cooked in honey.

T'FILLIN. A small square box containing a thin strip of parchment with inscription of text from Jewish law; worn on the left hand and forehead by Jewish males during the morning prayer on weekdays.

TORAH. Literally, the law. The Pentateuch or "Five Books of Mosese." The first five books of the Old Testament Bible.

YOM KIPPUR. The Day of Atonement; tenth and last day of the High Holy Days.

About The Author

LORRAINE GERSTL grew up in Johannesburg, South Africa. After graduating from the University of South Africa, she taught deaf children before starting her own family. She was active in Jewish Women's Organizations in South Africa before emigrating to the United States in 1976. Once established in Carmel, California, she became active as editor of the synagogue newspaper, *The Shofar*, and has been Vice President of Congregation Beth Israel. In 1988, she returned to teaching and now teaches third grade full-time at Santa Catalina School in Monterey. Her writing has been published in the Journal of California Teachers of English. She and her husband have five grown children.

The Millennium Publishing Group

Bon Vivant Press • Samuel Wachtman's Sons • Millennium Books

P.O. Box 1994
Monterey, CA 93942
800-524-6826 / 408-373-4499
FAX: 408-373-3567

Send _____ copies of *Jewish Cooking Secrets From Here & Far* at $14.95 each.

Send _____ copies of *How to Survive—And Profit From—Your Son's Bar Mitzvah* at $9.95 each.

Send _____ copies of *Tulio's Orange Tree* at $12.95 each.

Send _____ copies of *Pacific Northwest Cooking Secrets* at $15.95 each.

Send _____ copies of *Cooking Secrets for Healthy Living* at $15.95 each.

Send _____ copies of *The Gardener's Cookbook* at $15.95 each.

Send _____ copies of *The Great Vegetarian Cookbook* at $14.95 each.

Send _____ copies of *The Great California Cookbook* at $14.95 each.

Send _____ copies of *California Wine Country Cooking Secrets* at $13.95 each.

Send _____ copies of *San Francisco's Cooking Secrets* at $13.95 each.

Send _____ copies of *Monterey's Cooking Secrets* at $13.95 each.

Send _____ copies of *New England's Cooking Secrets* at $14.95 each.

Send _____ copies of *Cape Cod's Cooking Secrets* at $14.95 each.

Add $3.00 postage and handling for the first book ordered and $1.50 for each additional book. Please add $1.08 sales tax per book, for those books shipped to California addresses.

Please charge my ☐ Visa
☐ MasterCard # _____

Expiration date _____ Signature _____

Enclosed is my check for _____

Name _____

Address _____

City _____ State _____ Zip _____

☐ This is a gift. Please send directly to:

Name _____

Address _____

City _____ State _____ Zip _____